FREE from FEAR

*Understanding Fear's Control Over Your Life
and Why Loving It Will Set You Free*

ANDREW HACKETT

Holland House
PUBLISHING

NEW YORK

FREE FROM FEAR
Copyright ©2017 Andrew Hackett

All rights reserved. No part of this book may be used or reproduced in any manner whatsoever without written permission except in the case of brief quotations embodied in critical articles or reviews.

For information contact:
HollandHousePublishing.com

ISBN: 978-0-692-94129-4
First Edition: September 2017

10 9 8 7 6 5 4 3 2 1

To Michelle,

*You showed me how much life had to offer.
You opened your heart, wrapped me in your wings and
trusted that the universe brought us together for good reason.*

*You are the bodhisattva.
The example I was searching for.*

Your faith in me gave me life... so I could give life to others.

CONTENTS

Preface 13

Introduction 19

1. My Somewhat Ordinary Life 29

2. Where It All Started 37

3. Time to Heal 45

4. When the Clouds Began to Clear 53

5. My Awakening 63

6. From Clarity Came Consciousness 75

7. Love and Fear 83

8. The Ego and Its Influence Over You 103

9. Living in the Practical World 117

10. Manifestation for the Busy Person 149

11. Some Takeaways for the Soul 163

12. Four Thoughts to Ponder 177

13. The Link Between Your Uniqueness
    and Your Purpose in Life 199

14. Before You Run Off to Save the World 219

About the Author 229

DISCLAIMER: This book provides the personal experiences and beliefs of the author. It is sold with the understanding that neither the author nor the publisher is engaged in rendering legal, accounting, medical, psychological, or other professional services. If legal or other professional advice is warranted, the services of an appropriate professional should be sought. Neither author nor publisher accepts any liability or responsibility to any person or entity with respect to any loss or damage alleged to have been caused, directly or indirectly, by the information, ideas, opinions or other content in this book. If you do not agree to these terms, you should immediately return this book for a full refund.

(Above based on a jointly-adopted declaration by American Publishers Association and American Bar Association.)

Preface

Hello.

Yes, you. I thought I would find you here. It is dark out; come towards the light where I can see you.

There... that's better.

You look cold. Are you O.K.?

It is good to see you here, holding these words in your hands. I am excited to have you here with me, exploring the questions of the heart. I knew you would come, because you have been searching. Searching for answers in an increasingly difficult to understand world, searching for why things don't quite fit, why nothing seems quite right anymore.

Don't worry, you are not alone. In fact, you have more

company than you realise. We are all out here searching in the cold night for the truth, together like children with a dim torchlight wondering how many more are out here, also searching - some confused, some frightened, but not knowing of what.

Every now and then I gain a glimpse of another's light and run through the misty darkness, tripping over my way, only to pick myself up, dust myself off, with the light now gone. I seek for the same reasons you seek. Life is not complete. Not yet. There is so much more in your heart to explore - like the little girl in the fairy garden. Eyes wide open, in awe at all there is to know, experience and feel.

I had been searching for over 20 years, like a superhero with no cause. Knowing that there was more, but not knowing what, or how or why. We are born with unconditional love in our heart, carefree wonder at every leaf and bug we come across. You feel that love like a memory, not knowing where it went. You know in your heart it is out there, but maybe you have yet to find it again. You can't remember where you misplaced it or even when.

Adulthood arrived with a desperation in your mind to grow up and be all that you can be, but somewhere along the way responsibility crept in, casting a dark shadow over your everyday and all that is left is the feeling of the cold night's wind biting into your cheeks.

PREFACE

You remember how Responsibility rode in during a warm summer evening, on horseback, all exotic and sexy. It looked great at the time, dazzling you with its appeal and beauty, with its promise of riches and eternal happiness. You became good friends, talking and drinking into the night with ideals and dreams of changing the world and being rich and famous.

While you drank through the summer you failed to notice that Responsibility brought its friends along; slowly, piece by piece, they arrived from the shadows. First Pride arrived alongside Envy. Good friends they became, finding a seat at your table, but also delivering false hope. Anger, Grief and Guilt arrived sometime throughout the winter, you can't even remember how or why, but soon they became ingrained in your everyday life. Before you knew it, you had lost hope of your childhood dreams - lost the ideals the endless summer brought with it, and suddenly you became stuck in a life you no longer understood.

Where did it all go, what happened?

Fear arrived... and it brought its faithful followers with it.

Don't stop there; your seeking of the truth has brought you here. It is not only just around the corner, it is within you. Within all of us. You just need to remember, not where you left it (it is already there) but more of what it all meant to you.

The truth is here. Take the time to enable it, to awaken your inner soul to the journey you have been seeking for some time now. The words within these pages don't so much contain the truth; but they, in fact, enable Your Truth. You will relate some of your truth to the words you find within these pages, and you will find some of it in other pages. But the journey you are about to embark on is the biggest adventure you will ever undertake. It will be hard work, not without its trips or falls; but if you take my hand I will guide you gently towards that bright light. As you begin to piece together aspects of your truth, it will enable you to better understand why you feel the way you do: why you feel uncertain, why you can feel such immense joy and why you feel like there is so much more to know and experience.

You chose to come here, open these pages and look within. This is the start... it has already begun. The train has left the station and you are safe, comfortable and warm. It is time to face your demons, whatever they shall be. Nothing is too great for us to handle... for I have a secret to share... and it is going to set you free.

"A long journey ahead awaits the awakened soul. But a journey is not without growth, as is life, but necessary; for the love the dedication provides to the soul is but thanks enough for the gift of the life itself."

The Wise Old Man

Introduction

In today's world, Fear is a player in everyone's experience. Conditions like anxiety and depression are commonplace. Anxiety and depression are prevalent in every cross section of society and the numbers are growing. The society we live in is becoming increasingly disconnected. Families are more widespread and less supportive. Places of work are less social and more focussed on commercial return. Making and maintaining key relationships in our lives is becoming nearly impossible. To add to that, technology interferes with our normal social patterns of behaviour to the point that the disconnection that we feel to those around us is now the new norm.

I believe that there has been a rise in a fear-driven culture we all experience. The evidence of this is all around us. The media pushes fear down our throats through every medium available to them to increase ratings. Governments push society's reliance on its services to control and increase votes. The medical industry uses fear- created diseases and ailments purely for profit. Is it any wonder that we are losing faith in the very institutions that we rely on for safety, better health and societal control when their very backbones are corrupted in search of power and profit?

We don't even need their fear-driven interruption - already our own ego-driven fear permeates every aspect of our lives, controlling us like puppets in a lunchtime matinee. We worry about our kids. We stress about work. We judge our own worth, if we are not already judging other people for what they are or are not doing. We complain and criticise because it is easier than finding the worth in another, or the value in society's collective worth. We all have bills to pay and not enough money to get by. We are loaded in debt with high mortgages, but still find credit cards to fill up with all the necessary Christmas luxuries. We still have to put food on the table and fill our lunchboxes. All of this is nothing compared to the ego's fear-driven control over our thoughts, feelings - the pervasive illness that fills our bodies.

What would you say if someone came to you and said that it doesn't need to be this way? That this fear-driven disconnection from all that is around you is, in fact, just an illusion? Well, it *is* an

INTRODUCTION

illusion. The disconnection that is very much a part of contemporary living is merely a state of mind, one that we have created of our own accord - sometimes quite deliberately.

I believe that you are connected to everything and everyone that is around you. All you need to do is remember a few simple principles, implement some simple changes in your life, and the universe will open in front of your very eyes - enabling the very happiness and freedom your heart desires. I know. I have lived it.

Years ago, I realised my life needed to change because fear controlled me. In fact, it paralysed me almost every day. It controlled every aspect of who I was, how I acted and what I was to become. It scared the life out of me. Literally.

Then one morning the sun rose for the last time. It was the last time I would see that sun in the same light, for later that day my life changed forever. The sun set on an era in my life that was forever behind me, and after the best night's sleep I have ever had, the sun rose brighter, warmer and clearer than ever before. It was a new sun of possibility, potentiality and abundance. Never again was I alone in the dark, searching in the cold dark night with a dim flashlight, batteries failing.

I had manifested love in my life: perfect unconditional love. I no longer felt fear and I was able to create whatever I wanted in my life. Realising this was a very profound, emotionally-charged experience for me. One I will never forget.

It wasn't without challenges, difficulties or error. All of it didn't happen overnight. But, as I later realised, challenges and mistakes will always exist in this physical world. That is the reason why we are here, the reason why we chose to live this life. But this time, for me, everything that happened was a blessing: every challenge, every lesson, every trial. A gift - and I was eternally grateful for it all.

I spent most of my life as a very self-aware person, and finally it was paying dividends - finally it was all making sense. My thirst for knowledge - for understanding and logically working through each and every process - was outshone only by the divine guidance that was bestowed upon me.

At first my ego took this and ran with it. I struggled with being worthy, and then I thought that not only was I worthy, but very special. I am special! But after coming down to earth I realised that I am no more special than you, or anyone else on the planet for that matter. What took me time to understand was not how, but *why*. Strangely enough, it was also the most obvious answer - my ability to see was clouded by my ego.

What time, patience and a profoundly gentle water-born energy showed me is that I am, in fact, no different to anyone; in fact, we are all the same. So much so that we are in fact all one. The

INTRODUCTION

great boss of the universe doesn't bestow favouritism on any one person - in fact there is no judgement imparted at all. We all have the ability to grow, to understand and to free ourselves of the painful bondage that is our physical existence.

When I woke up to myself I started to *see* for the first time. I noticed the pain and suffering of those around me, the insanity experienced by nearly everyone I came across. It wasn't through judgement, it was compassion, as I tried to understand. I realised that people live with fear every day. It controls them, it consumes them and it poisons them. It creates disease and illness in their lives, both mental and physical.

In realising what is happening all around us, I also realised that we are in control of our destiny. We do manifest our day-to-day experience. It didn't take long to understand that our very thoughts are the creative mechanism that signals to the universe what our desires are. Every thought, every action we undertake are tools for creating our future experience.

Now you need to understand: there are no miracles in my story. I don't come from a spiritually gifted heritage and my upbringing was normal in every way. I had a profound experience that I believe was divinely provided. That experience led me to read, extensively, and to search out teachers for guidance and direction. I also decided to focus on myself, find time to meditate, and travel away to find my inner truth and search for the answers to the many questions that plagued me. I cannot take all the credit for what I learned because I believe the universe was intent on me learning specific things that quickly came together to make sense. Books landed in my lap to read. People showed up to give me messages. I started to recognise the synchronicities in daily life and to listen to the instructions that they gave me.

Now I need to be clear here: I am in no position to tell you how to live your life; in fact, I don't believe anyone is. I am not perfect and I don't have all the answers. I am very human in every way. However, I do believe that what I offer you within these pages can help free you from your daily fears and teach you how to keep the ego at bay.

Some of what you read in this book will resonate with you and some may not. You may find answers in other books, old and new (as I did), and that may also feel like your truth. I suggest to anyone that you should always follow your intuition on what to read and when to listen. Your intuition is the key - listen to it and separate it from your thoughts. This isn't easy at first, but I can show you.

Within the following pages I will show you how to connect to your intuition, what to listen for, so you can recognise how fear presents in your life and what methods it uses to control you. I will give you tools to use to help you understand your fears and to

INTRODUCTION

enable fear to fall away from your day-to day-life. I hope that from the journey we take, and through practicing the techniques discussed within these pages, you will not only conquer your fears, but also learn to understand the role your thoughts play in manifesting all the events around you that you experience as everyday life.

The tools you will learn to understand and to practice can be done anytime, anywhere - whether you are a busy mother, a hard worker, a student or a teacher.

I believe that with the right guidance, and with a bit of courage to look at things in a different way, the point where you master your fears will become the most incredible experience of your life, producing such extraordinary happiness and joy that you will want to share it with the world - just as I am doing with you right now.

I now know that what we think, how we think, and the resulting behaviours it influences in any given moment, *is* what defines us. I discovered through years of research, learning and experience that how we relate to every moment determines how the moment interrelates with us. What we send out to the universe through our thoughts, our actions, and our behaviours is soaked up by the greater universe and sent back to us ten-fold.

I have learned to accept that we are all creators of our own destiny; we are all capable of shaping the way the universe interacts with us. So much so that we can soon manifest anything and everything our heart truly desires.

Through the process of learning to understand the way the universe works, I realised that the fear, anxiety and depression that influences vast portions of society is not only unnecessary but we can, in fact, switch it off entirely. We can control precisely how much influence fear has in our day-to-day lives. By changing the way we think we can determine how happy we are, how successful we are, and most importantly: what our destiny becomes.

In this book, I will break this all down for you. I will help you identify where fear controls you and what tools it uses to do so. More importantly, I will provide you with the tools you need to remove fear from your life altogether and show you how magnificent you and your life can really be.

If you are tired of living in fear, constantly anxious about everything going on in your life, join me and let me open your mind and your heart. The universe has put this book in your hands for a reason. So buckle in, find a comfy seat and prepare yourself for the change of a lifetime.

On the other side of fear's door is Love. Infinite, unconditional Love. It is beautiful, warm and friendly. It creates abundance, happiness and peace in your life, and it will connect

INTRODUCTION

you to others, to the earth, and to the universe.

My journey, from an infant to the man you see before you, has been somewhat ordinary - not one of privilege or sacrifice. But a life, nonetheless, of meaning and uncertainty.

What I learned as a child didn't prepare me as a teenager.

For the peaceful soul needs to be challenged. As the stone is nothing without the sculptor's chisel, so life is nothing without the growth we experience through pain.

What I experienced as a teenager, didn't prepare me for adulthood. But betrayal and suffering are but two of many tools the universe uses to sculpt our story.

Each story must have a beginning, even if it does not yet end.

Chapter One

My Somewhat Ordinary Life

I was born late in December in the year of 1973 in Canberra, Australia. I chose Barbara and Alan as my parents; and as it turns out, I also chose my older siblings, Simon and Peter. I was raised in a typical middle-class family home in the outer suburbs of Northern Canberra, for what was a reasonably normal, matter-of-fact, happy childhood.

I have many fond memories of my childhood, going back as far as when I was two years old. The day my mother accidentally left me behind at her friend's house, a new house without landscaped yards. I had friends to play with until she realised she only had two in the back seat. I wasn't that perturbed. I also remember playing cars with my friends amongst the roots of an old tree at my preschool in Melbourne and having sleepovers with school friends in primary school.

Overall my childhood was normal - whatever that is supposed to mean. It was a happy, supportive childhood without the many challenges faced by other children in the world. I was an imaginative and creative child with two doting older brothers who would strategically seek my support in their own battle of wits. Not a bad position for a three-year-old to be in.

Throughout my childhood I remembered being a contented child, with a confidence brought on by my affectionate mother, who still treats me as her baby boy to this day. My father was a quiet, reserved man who not only relished in simple activities like listening to his BBC radio programs, but was a great (yet firm) teacher. Neither of my parents ever left me wanting.

Growing up was even more normal. Like most kids I guess, I found myself constantly dreaming of flying in my sleep, I remember it so fondly. I made friends easily, but one day I found myself beating up the school bully in year nine during a prearranged fight on the school oval on Friday afternoon. I was O.K. at school, and even though my studies lacked dedication, I

CHAPTER ONE

cruised through nonetheless.

Overall, I was a helpful, kind kid of old-world culture and chivalry who loved to support the underdog. I established a core group of friends - not many, but long- lasting.

I was always adept at understanding others: knowing when they hurt, feeling their concern and empathising with their situation. Although a little awkward socially (in that I wouldn't always know what to say - particularly to girls), I apparently seemed to enable others to feel better, stronger, more capable. I would give strength to others when they needed it most, and protect them when that wasn't enough.

As a teenager, I had typical problems and many questions. I struggled to understand the spiritual influence in my life, but knew the Church didn't sit right for me. With parents of strong faith, I struggled with the concept of control that the Church's teachings espoused. This was confirmed for me with the unexpected sexual abuse I suffered at the hands of a teacher from my Catholic school. I didn't know it at the time, but I was one of many; and I didn't know that the school knew and failed to act. It wasn't until much later, when I decided to confront the demons it created in my heart, that I realised that the Church not only knew about the abuse, but possibly sanctioned it through inaction and cover-ups.

I developed a Guardian role early in my life. I would see

myself as some kind of superhero, even though I did not understand what my role was, nor what secret powers I was supposed to possess. I once found a friend in the schoolyard with both his wrists and thighs slashed. I felt like I should have been able to stop it before it happened. I finally received some clarity when a psychologist explained the inherited guardianship role I had been born with, a role that – I later realised – had carried with me over many lifetimes.

The clarity in recognising my inherited guardianship role was incredible. For the first time I had a glimpse of my future role in this universe, but I wasn't able to grasp it completely, nor understand it, for another twenty years.

What I did know at this time was that information came to me easily. I felt it was real when it would fall in my lap at the precise time I needed it. My memory has always been exceptional, but not a gift of brilliance by any means. I knew I could understand things easily, but only in the context of the world as I understood it at that point in time. Back then, I really had no idea of the way the universe worked. None at all.

Like a cat, I always landed on my feet - and I still do to this day. My father has always struggled to understand how I got so far in my career, so young; and, how I managed to earn so well throughout my 20s and 30s. I had many jobs: some real, some not

CHAPTER ONE

so much. Although I enjoyed university, I realised half way through that a creative occupation was not for me, as I didn't enjoy my results when working under pressure. My creativity was a gift I used to help me relax, and, as it happens, has resulted in some beautiful gardens that I built from the ground up.

Through my years at university I found that my creative side was strong but the output suffered when I had to produce quality results under pressure. It was at his point that I thought that my day job needed to be black-and-white, not something creative. Boy, did I get that wrong! But it has been an honest living. A desk job that paid the bills, and paid them well; a job that enabled me to set up the foundation of my life's work, unknowingly, unwittingly. It didn't harm others, wasn't corrupt or morally questionable, but it also didn't help others or change things for the better. It always left me feeling empty - like a superhero with no cause.

I met my future wife around my twentieth birthday. We were young and crazy, like most twenty-something's in the '90s. We became good friends and established a strong and loving eighteen-year relationship. She was a great friend to me and helped me through many dark times. Mostly by just being there, or by being herself; sometimes through knowing what I needed and when I needed it. She is a giving soul, working selflessly as a nurse, and in her own way, helping others heal. We married in Sydney in 2001 and set forth on a happy path that saw our two boys, Jamie and Sam, come into this world. I am so glad my boys chose us as parents. They are great boys, kind, loving and fun to be around. We laugh a lot – which, as it turns out, has been the best therapy for all concerned.

We separated in early 2012. It was harder than I ever expected but now I am thankful, because although we were always great friends, we can now also be happier on our own journeys, at peace to revel in all things that life has to offer.

My journey (like all journeys, I believe) has been a series of synchronistic events that have governed my life. I don't believe my story is special, or overly unique; though I do believe that it has happened through divine intervention and has a purpose that is not only beyond my understanding, but is happening for reasons that are also beyond me as the individual. It is as though the events in my life are happening not for me, but through me... for others.

I am just a piece in the overall puzzle of life, like you are - but we need to remember that a puzzle is not complete with a missing piece. You are just as important to humanity as I am, as is your own awakening. In fact, I will go so far as to say that you are just as important to humanity as has anyone else ever has been. The great humans of our history were ordinary humans, too. I believe that the only real difference was that, when the opportunity arose

CHAPTER ONE

for them, they were present enough to listen to their moment of great inspiration and courageous enough to follow it.

I dream that this story will resonate with all the people who read it. Many of you might not feel that you are here to save the world or to save humanity, but I do believe you feel, in some way or another, that you are here to make a difference.

I do hope this book shows you that great things are not only possible, but they are already happening within each and every one of us. Collectively we already have the power to save the world. To save humanity from itself. We just need to better understand our role - which piece of the great puzzle of life that represents us - and have the courage to do what is necessary to participate. Because without our piece of the puzzle, other pieces may not be able to happen.

I am not talking about taking swift action, running through the streets with placards, uprising against evil, or overthrowing governments. I am talking about the little things in life that create possibility. I am talking about the seeds that grow forests. It is something that you can do from where you are at this precise moment - where you are at anytime, doing anything. It is about the realisation that you are already capable. It is already within you.

When I decided to "fix myself" in July 2007, little did I know at the time what that meant. I had no idea what I was to do, how or really even why. All I knew was that I deserved so much more - and that those around me deserved more, too.

I was right. I just had no idea how much I was right.

Chapter Two

Where It All Started

For almost 20 years I suffered at the hands of a sexual predator. It only happened once, when I was fifteen years old. But the betrayal, shame, guilt and self-loathing almost destroyed me many times over. I changed from a light-hearted, life-loving teenager to a dark, angry young man. It was a well-kept secret for almost 20 years - not even my closest friend suspected what had happened. She honestly had no idea. But she put up with my troubled ways for 18 years, like only good friends do.

I used drugs and alcohol to numb me down and to relax my troubled mind. Some days my self-abuse was heavier than others, but I became very adept at keeping the cause of this shame to myself. I learned to control those around me - but not in the aggressive sense of the word, because I never wanted to be an abuser. I could never forgive myself for that. The control of others was always intended in a friendly, self-preservation kind of way, but (I must admit) not always received in that context.

I realised sometime after 2001 that I wasn't the only victim of his evil ways. This was after my abuser took his own life after a 20-year trail of sexual abuse caught up with him. The police got involved and he ran and hid in a car like a coward. Hose to the tailpipe. Parked in the forest. Even though his death was met with a smile on my young face, it failed to last long. I realised that had I reported my incident, it may have stopped him in his tracks twelve years earlier.

Guilt was added to my relentless shame. I started to understand the past trail of suicides that followed the abuser and piece together the long list of lies that also followed. I learned that some of the school's teachers tried to raise the alarm, but they were ignored by the school and its authority, the Church. This created further anger in my heart that took years to understand.

But over the years, much self-examination showed me that there were always two underlining powers at play deep within my psyche.

First, I hated being out of control of my body and my environment. I preferred clean tidy surroundings, as I learned to

CHAPTER TWO

garden my outdoor space to beautify it, despite living in a concrete jungle. I enjoyed meditative activities like vacuuming and mowing lawns and was always picking up after others around me. When I would drink, I would rarely get drunk, unless I was in the safety of my own home. I hated the thought that my drunkenness could put me in that situation again. In fact, I immediately stayed clear of any situation that would weaken my defences. It was always a balancing act with alcohol - wanting to disconnect from the world, but remaining capable enough to ensure I wouldn't allow any harm to come to me or my loved ones. My need to control my space and those around me was a subconscious action, repeated because it made me feel calmer, even though it was a false alternative to peace. Strangely enough, it never helped me either way.

Second, I had an unrelenting desire to make something of myself - to pick myself up and brush myself off. The old saying that constantly sat like a parrot on my shoulder was, "It is not why we fall that matters; it is how we pick ourselves up that defines us." I refused to allow my past to define me, to control my future output, to determine my forward path; yet I struggled with the constant reminder of my shame and failure as a teenager, my guilt, and the association I had with my victim identity. I lived a constant battle of fear and anxiety and I allowed it to control me. Again, another balancing act that never got me to where I wanted to be.

For some unknown reason I always knew I was destined for bigger things - possibly for great things, perhaps even for success. From quite a young age I knew, with some sense of certainty, that I was destined for something great. What I was unclear about though was: how, and through what means would my success arrive? Like the crow of the cockerel at first light, the reminder constantly reassured me and kept me just strong enough not to let go and succumb to the shadow of shame and guilt that followed me.

But it was never success in the traditional image. From the age of twelve all I ever wanted was my own space, a house, a garden and family to share it with. It was never a picture of success in the Tony Robbins sense of the word. It was never about celebrity, money or fast cars. It was subtler than that. It was just a feeling, undeniable and unrelenting. It is still present to this very day. Little did I know at this point that success is all relative. It means different things to different people. Success to me at this point in my life meant *peace*. Internal Peace.

Alas, I had much to learn. I needed to experience pain, heartache and love. I needed to contribute to the continuity of humanity to see its resounding beauty, and it was through that angelic beauty that I realised that enough was enough. As I started

CHAPTER TWO

to put my ego behind me and understand that I had it all wrong, I was visited by two Angels, both beautiful and each bearing a message. Both created visceral reactions in me, pounding hard on my heart, reaching down into my stomach to pull it through my throat, each unrelenting, unforgiving and delivering a message I needed to hear. I now believe they were sent from the universe, from the Angels themselves. I just didn't know it at the time.

The first Angel took the form of my eldest son, Jamie. Barely three years of age at the time, he was such an unrelenting source of joy for me. His smile was that of the golden age of Atlantis: pure, good, and direct from the Source itself. His introduction into my life is so clear in my mind. The time spent on the floor, watching with unworthy amazement, was a gift from the heavens, joyfulness at its root cause. He gave me more life than anything else ever had, made me realise what a fool I had become, and what wasted time my life had been up until then. But what was next?

Then she appeared. The Angel in my dreams. Short, petite, without wings. Always the same dream, short and to the point, delivered with stage-like direction, tearful as a Shakespearian tragedy. Curly dark hair to the neckline, wearing panties and a bra, with her hands on my bare chest. Myself in jeans, facing each other, with short lit clouds all around and darkness beyond. Looking up at me with nothing but pure love, she would say, "Have no fear. All will be O.K. I am here." Then nothing.

The cold, darkened bedroom would greet me from my startled awakening. At first my heart would pound, sweaty, confused, almost alarmed. Who was this woman, this Angel? What did it all mean? What is going on here?

The second night's dream turned into three. Then four, a week, and then a month. Every night she would visit - the same dream, the same words, the same unrelenting love. It was pure, unconditional and no doubt from a higher being, but for what? Why? I started to search for her in my pre-sleep wakefulness, and sure enough, she always arrived. Beauty beyond earthly bounds, but undoubtedly deliberate.

Then anxiety would rush me to my feet, make me lightheaded and sick to the stomach. The message from Jamie would arrive soon, but first I had to understand what was happening. Each evening the routine of the household was firm but wonderful. Playtime, bath time, dinnertime, quiet time then bedtime. A routine that worked well for all. There is no sleep like that of a well-fed, clean, warm baby that is loved and secure.

My boy was an avid bottle drinker and required a nappy change late at night around 10:30 p.m. to stop him over filling his nappy to bursting point. Since I was a bit of a night owl I always got the job. Each night I watched his innocence lying on the bed,

CHAPTER TWO

fast asleep in his angelic beauty, and worried that *what had happened to me might one day happen to him*. It made me sick to the bone, violently ill. I couldn't move past it. The feeling would overpower me to the point that I would leave the room, nappy changed, and throw up.

After almost three months of her visiting me in my dreams, and weeks of escalating anxiety over a simple nappy change, she visited once more. Her hands on my chest, petite and beautiful. Same as before. She said, "Have no fear. All will be O.K. I am here. It's time for you to heal." She stood on her tippy toes and placed an ever-so-gentle kiss on my lips. And I never saw her in my dreams again.

The next morning, my life changed forever.

Chapter Three

Time to Heal

This morning was forever to be known as the morning that changed everything. I had never told a soul about my abuser, but I knew it was time to get it off my chest. It was time to deal with this once and for all. For the sake of my boys, for the sake of my family. For my own sake.

I was hoping to feel relieved and empowered; instead, I was frightened. Recent news articles of pending legal cases of other abused students from my school were all across the newspapers of the day. I wasn't afraid of the accused - he was long dead, and maybe he was chatting to the big boss to gain entry into heaven, so to speak. Or maybe he didn't care either way.

I was scared about how I would tell my wife. I had kept that secret for at least fifteen years by this stage. I didn't keep any secrets other than that, as I never felt the need. How was she going to respond? Honestly, I was terrified.

I wasn't sure how to bring it up. I didn't know what to say. How do you start a conversation like that? We were watching the television, and on the news was a local story about the court cases some were embarking on to seek recompense: maybe an apology, maybe some answers. Plaintiffs were suing the Church, the school and the individual people in those places of authority who failed to do anything, and in fact had allowed it to happen. How they slept at night was always a question I pondered.

Finally, I told my wife what happened over fifteen years earlier; and to be honest, she was relieved. Saddened, but relieved. Troubled, but relieved. It explained so much: my behaviour, my alcoholism, my shifting from job to job, our relationship together, and its shortfalls. My moods and my troubled ways. She was relieved because she had somehow blamed herself for my ways. It was never her guilt to carry; she only helped, in her gentle way, to keep me safe from myself. It was a role she thankfully performed for many years without knowing. I didn't tell anyone else… none of my friends or family. They didn't need to know.

My parents wondered. They even asked over the years. I lied to them because I know they would have blamed themselves for letting me go with him on that day. I lied to them because of the

CHAPTER THREE

shame I carried for not being strong enough at the time. I lied to them because I wanted to protect them from my pain. The fact was, I was 15 years old and no one was ever going to tell me what to do. I never told them because it was never their fault (not even mine, for that matter) and I never wanted to cause them the suffering they would have put themselves through. Lying is not something for me to apologise for; it was self-preservation. I think nearly everyone I know who was also abused lied, too - to protect their loved ones and to hide the shame that destroyed their very sense of self-worth. I lied to protect my parents; and although I now know it wasn't the best choice to have made at the time, because they love me so much, I know they do understand.

I made an appointment to visit the lawyer to set things straight. I wanted to share my information with him to help the other cases that were happening. I felt that if I could only redress my guilt of not reporting it decades earlier, for not saying something to stop this monster, then the guilt might disappear. At the time, of course, I didn't know there were others. I honestly had no idea. But when I found out, many years after, the guilt awoke like an evil beast, ready to destroy me.

The sense of relief in me was obvious. I had finally gotten it off my chest - I had finally released those dragons of self-harm and internal judgement into the ether to be free and fly amongst the angels. It did feel great, but it also brought with it a new problem: How the hell was I going to do all this?

I needed help. I had a great friend to be there with me, but I needed professional help - someone trained to help me understand, someone to talk to that wouldn't judge, that wouldn't push me, that wouldn't punish me.

I visited a couple of psychologists. Both helped in one way or another. They assisted me with understanding that it wasn't my fault, or my wrongdoing. I was not to blame for this monster's action. But there was no Holy Grail, no lightbulb moment that solved all my woes. Only a gentle and gradual process of self-help and guidance.

Now, to anyone reading this, I must say it is imperative to seek professional help to deal with your past issues. Releasing those demons within is a highly liberating experience, but it is still important to address our past problems and not continue to cover them up with all the excuses and reframing we come up with. Please reach out and make the change that is necessary for you to grow. There are people around, and programs to help, with the process. I know it isn't easy. But be aware that we all have demons, skeletons in the closet. The greatest realisation is that those that matter to you - your true, heartfelt friends - will not judge you or think less of you. They will support you and be there when you

CHAPTER THREE

need it. Ultimately, it is you that needs to be there for yourself. This process is not about receiving the answer, or the apology; it is really about forgiving yourself, loving yourself, and truly believing in your very core that you are worth fighting for; and at the very least, getting it out and off your chest. It is easily the best feeling in the world, and it can easily become the most liberating experience of your life.

For me, the process of healing was not what I expected. It was easier than I had ever thought possible. For something that was the most difficult thing I will ever face in my life, that's a strange thing to realise. (It was like when we procrastinate about something we don't want to do, but know we have to do. It is never as hard, as difficult or as time consuming as we built it up to be in our minds.) But did I realise it at the time? No, certainly not; but looking back, I suppose everything appears easier than it was.

The healing didn't come from the psychological help, although that was important and a great deal of understanding came from it that was essential to the process. The healing didn't come from the legal process, either. I must say, that was a farce. Lawyers fighting with lawyers. What a joke that was. They tried to sympathise, even empathise, but always with barbed tongues. They didn't send a priest, or a minister, or even a counsellor to greet me. They sent their insurance company's lawyer… and they have the hide to tell us how to live our lives.

Why is it that the Church and its so-called leaders think they have anything to teach the world through their corrupt control of humanity? Controlling people through fear and lies! Even their interpretation of their so-called God is so blatantly corrupt. I am sorry if this offends some people who, in reading this, feel I am attacking their belief system. I honestly do not intend to do so. Rather, it is the corporation I strongly object to - the organisation that controls through fear and oppression - that makes me feel violently ill and angry. I am not just speaking of any one religion either. They all call you sinners and then hold out their hand for your money. They can even direct debit your bank account to make the corruption easier for their followers to participate in. But this story isn't to bash the Church; they are more than capable of creating their own demise. Enough said.

The legal process was where I (rather wrongly) thought I would find an apology. That was my first mistake, but also my first lesson. It wasn't until I realised that my healing, my internal growth on this matter, had surpassed the legal process that I realised I couldn't move further forward. The legal process was keeping me in that pain body, reminding me of the pain, and therefore I had to cut it loose.

There was never an apology. There was never going to be.

CHAPTER THREE

Why I thought hearing an apology from my abuser and those who failed to protect me from him was going to help, let alone arrive, was simply delusional. This led me to ask myself, "Why do we need an authoritarian figure to tell us something is true to believe it? Why do we seek their approval of our beliefs? Who are they to us?"

As we grow up we often develop our own belief system, sometimes in contrast to our parents or our friends' beliefs. But do we seek their approval to believe in it? No, often we don't. So why would we seek the approval of a stranger, or (least of all) from an organisation that we know are abusers, liars and hypocrites? Suddenly it sounds a little silly... doesn't it?

So I dumped the legal process. Cut my losses and moved on. It was never going to help me, and my evidence was on the record should it be required to help others. Suddenly I felt free - and this is where the wounds really started to heal. The healing came from my simple change of mind, my decision to stop associating my self-worth, my story, to the pains in my past and to start associating it to the exciting unknown path ahead. I finally had a chance to reinvent myself: to create who I wanted to be and what I wanted to be known for. It was the most extraordinary feeling, the most beautiful release from my bonded chains.

For the first time, I was free. I was free of my guilt, free of my pain and self-judgement on that matter. The world opened up for me, and it was then - some two or three years after that crippling fear of being powerless to protect my newborn son - that I now identify as the turning point for me. Free of self-judgement.

The healing came from me letting it all go. Not the legal process; that was just a mechanism. I mean letting go of my judgement of others, of myself, or the life I was dealt and more importantly, just letting go. Realising that I was identifying my self- worth and my self-value with what others were thinking: their actions, their beliefs. That was wrong. What do I care if they are sorry for their wrongdoing? Why should I identify my happiness with that? With them? Why would I allow anyone else to influence my self-worth, my emotional safety, and my happiness? I knew I was worth fighting for. Worth loving.

I was just learning to undertake the process of taking my hands off the wheel and realising, "It will all be O.K" I was at the cusp of believing in my core that I can survive anything - that it is my belief, my faith in myself, that not only matters most, but is, in fact, the single driving force the will open up the universe at my feet. I was free to grow, reach my arms out wide, as far as they could go, and see what the universe had in mind for me.

I remember it well. It was truly beautiful. More than a turning point. A new life.

What now? I asked myself... and the silence was deafening.

Chapter Four

When the Clouds Began to Clear

Well, the next step was a bit of a cliché, but one worth doing nonetheless. I mean what do people do when they have the opportunity to start anew? What do they reach for when given such an uplifting opportunity? For me, it was about getting back to basics, creating simplicity in my life, breaking everything down to its raw form and evaluating its worth as a healthy contributor in my life.

I did what any crazy person would do in such a situation.

I bought a farm.

I know, you are either thinking I was really mad, or thinking, "What's so bad about that?" Either way you are probably right. That's what my friends thought.

FREE FROM FEAR

They said, "What do you know about cattle?" How will you live? What about the family?" And they were right. I didn't know anything about farming life. I didn't know how it was all going to turn out. And that excited me. But I did know that everything would be O.K. For the first time in my life I felt like I was on track. Towards what, I had no idea. But it felt right.

The farm was in a very small village called Tilba Tilba on the New South Wales South Coast in Australia. It is a very special little farm - 60 acres of rolling green hills, only three kilometres from the coastline and nestled in the womb of our beautiful Mother Gulaga.

Mother Gulaga is an ancient mountain, known by the Europeans as Mount Dromedary. Once a 3000-metre-high volcanic mountain, her eruption several millennia ago resulted in her giving birth to her two sons, Najanuga (Little Mt. Dromedary) and Baranguba (Montague Island).

Mother Gulaga is very sacred to the local indigenous Yuin People. In fact, to the Yuin people, Gulaga is a sacred mother, just as Uluru (Ayres Rock, in Alice Springs) is a sacred father. The farm sits right between the Mother and her baby. As you can imagine, the energy between the two is strong, protective and (for the unconscious) overpowering. At this point I understood the basics about the mountain. I certainly didn't understand her energy, her

CHAPTER FOUR

requirements of me living in her space, or what she had in store for me. I certainly had no idea of what was ahead, nor was I aware that my Angels where in cahoots with her all along.

My understanding of the Divine's plan didn't arrive until some years later. In fact, the first year was a bit of a blur. I worked in Canberra three days per week while trying to raise a family, keep a farm under control, make the required improvements, and keep the changes within me to some manageable speed. As you may expect, it was a lot to manage and take on board. My marriage suffered, and then broke.

That was when I started on a downward spiral that nearly broke *me*. Without a doubt, this was the hardest, most emotional path I have ever been on. Difficult, because our two boys were caught up in it all. But I will say, because we were both focussed on what was right for the kids, we managed this very difficult situation that minimised the pain the kids shared. We soon saw a return to their joyful, chatty natures we had grown to love. I now understand that this whole process of separation was one of my biggest learning curves. To learn to love where there is pain; to be kind where there is anger; and to do what is right, despite all the heartache, all the guilt and all the difficult hurdles.

That year was a year of extraordinary personal exploration, a journey through the jungle of unknown purpose. It was a battle of complex paths and painful challenges, all the while trying to laugh because that's what the kids needed to see. Looking back at it now, it was a very personal journey of great consequences. Searching internally through thick fog, not understanding what was on the other side, not even really knowing what I wanted to see past the fog. Just knowing, with blind faith, that it was necessary for all involved.

The details of this are very personal. Private in fact - and out of respect for my ex-wife and good friend, I won't detail it. But I feel I need to clarify that only after great rain does the sun shine its brightest. Only after great darkness can the warmth of the light be truly felt. I don't mean to devalue this period of my life. It was as important as any period was and will be, but it was a turning point. A moment that was needed. A moment of reflection. I am in no doubt that, without it, what happened next couldn't have happened, as that was when the clouds began to clear.

Now let me be clear: this was well before I could see, let alone understand - and in my opinion at the time, well before I was worthy. My own feeling of worthiness was a complex issue for me, as it lay on the ground like a residual carcass of shame rotting on the forest floor. I hadn't identified any real self-worth at this point, so I could not accept me being worthy of anything that ever happened to me. If the shame of my past had finally passed, it was

CHAPTER FOUR

soon replaced with the shame of my failed marriage. I soon realised that I hadn't learned what I needed to learn. I wasn't ready to accept... but that was the point. My spirit guides had a plan; time was of the essence, and it was time for a jolt. A wake-up call - and as you may already know, they have their ways, and their ways are always effective when they intend them to be. I didn't know this then, but boy was I about to find out!

And that's when it happened. Out of the blue, without notice, my Angel visited me once again... but this time I wasn't dreaming.

It was mid-morning in September - a fresh Canberra day in the early-but-definite stages of Spring. I always loved Spring. It has always been a significant time of the year for me. It was the rebirth each year that I later enjoyed as an avid gardener, and then more literally, as a farmer. Spring is pure and divine - an unconditional love offered by Mother Nature each year, necessary for the cycle of life, and for our mental health. It always feels like she forgives us for our sins, replenishes the resources after her hard winter, and fills our hearts with abundant wonder.

Sitting with a cup of tea at a café near my work, I glanced over my shoulder to see a beautiful woman standing some 20 metres away. She looked strangely familiar, but the reflection from the glass-panelled windows between us could not disguise my need to stare. Strangely familiar, but from where? A better look helped clarify. Within seconds my heart leaped out of my chest. I turned back and sat deeper into my chair. The blood had rushed from my head to my heart. Dizzy, unbelieving.

This worthiness issue had raised its ugly head for me once again. I didn't understand my divine connection; in fact, none of it made sense to me at all. I didn't understand a lot as it turned out - and soon I was to be reminded of that. I didn't understand. Were my eyes tricking me? Was I seeing things?

With my back to her now I tried my best to hide… but each time I looked over my shoulder I found her smiling. A cheeky, knowing smile. A loving smile. I panicked. This couldn't be! She was the one in my dreams - my Angel that reassured me for many months that it was O.K. to move forward, to start the healing process some five years earlier. Wait, was she real? Was I seeing something that wasn't really there?

I turned around to verify, to understand the answers to these questions. But she was gone. I rose from my chair and left my table with a glazed look on my face. Where did she go? What just happened? Was she real? Too many questions.

A sleepless night followed. What did all this mean? Was any of it real? I didn't understand, but I wanted to so much. I closed my eyes over and over reliving the dreams I had had many years ago, trying to hold on to something that happened too fast earlier

CHAPTER FOUR

that day. The next day's sun rose - another beautiful day, but with so many questions and so few answers.

I saw her again on this new day. Then the next. And then the next. She *was* real. Physical. Not a dream. She was perfect in fact. Beautiful. She was REAL!!! I had no idea what to make of this at all, but I wasn't complaining. Lightning had struck me and wanted it to keep striking me, over and over and over, because it felt so damned good.

Each time we saw each other, she smiled. I grew to love that stunning, cheeky smile of hers. Different from the dream. That was loving, caring and divine. Heavenly. But I didn't understand what was happening. This didn't seem right. Since my separation I hadn't looked at any others. I wasn't interested. I wasn't ready. After nine months I wasn't sure what the appropriate time period one was to respect their ex-partner after 18 years. But I couldn't stop thinking about my Angel. I looked forward to going to work with the thought that I would bump into her. She consumed me. Things happened within my body that I had never felt before. This was more than love - I had been in love before, a couple of times. This was different. This was physical. This was spiritual. It was pure bliss. When she smiled, her whole being smiled, the room brightened, and the earth slowed down just a bit. It was like all living things collectively, although unconsciously, wanted to savour that moment with me; as if, through our combined divine power, we could make that smile last a few seconds longer - and in doing so, the world was definitely a better place. I noticed her security badge and her name: *Michelle*. For weeks I hadn't even been able to notice or remember what she was like below the neckline. That smile cast spells on me and I walked around, clumsily bumping into things. Then along came the Wise Old Man.

Of course, as unconscious as I was then, I didn't recognise synchronistic events until much later, and the more obscure they were, the longer it would take to see the connections. But he arrived, bold and sure. Confident and old-worldly, and boy could he write.

He could cast his own spells in the words he used. Little did I know that he was also in cahoots with my Angels. Little did I know they were all in cahoots with her Angels, that there was a master plan being orchestrated that is far beyond both of us mere mortals. It is a master plan that involves great things, thousands of beings, and hundreds of thousands of Angels. Two lifetimes had come together - a plan of generations of work culminating at this one point. The Wise Old Man knew it; he knew everything. This was the moment that *had* to happen.

So I drafted an email. It was poetry in every sense of the word.

CHAPTER FOUR

I figured out where she worked. I sent it. A very modern meeting, caused by the fact that each time I was near her energy field my knees wouldn't work properly, my mouth wouldn't close, and my heart wouldn't stop leaping out of my chest as if to try and embrace her own. Despite being a confident, together type of guy, she was my kryptonite. My ultimate weakness. Little did I know, I was also hers. The email seemed like the sensible thing to do.

Because of the feelings we stirred in each other, we opted to share a few emails between us before we gained the courage to meet in person. She even went on holiday for two weeks before returning for us to meet in person. This is where the Wise Old Man performed his magic.

I later understood that I was channelling his magical words. I remember writing emails as if in a semi-trance. I would type as fast as I could, and never correct my words. What came out was beyond me - old-worldly. It was received by her as, "Our souls were talking to each other." She was reading my words, and her soul was celebrating with pure joy. Talking like she dared to talk, listening to words she dreamed of hearing. What I wrote was so true to her being, it even seemed at that stage as if we knew each other before - from another world, from another life. All this before we had even met.

And then we met. Wow! Only truth could be spoken; there

was no other language. Only love was felt, except when we touched, because sparks would pass between us. This was all so surreal, so unstoppable. It was as scary as it was extraordinary. It was as beautiful as it was predetermined. The Angels spared no expense in ensuring this was going to happen, and it most certainly did.

This was a path to learn to love each other unconditionally, as much as it was to learn to love ourselves unconditionally. Everything was perfect, peaceful and divine. We loved ourselves more from being together, whether we were in each other's company or not. Our pain bodies left us; fear fell away, and our ability to connect to the divine would become easier and easier in time. We had no idea what was ahead of us - two unawakened souls embarking on a journey of endless love and limitless possibilities. It was the rollercoaster to be on, but it seemed like we were the only two standing in line.

It is a bliss that lives on to this day, albeit quieter, gentler and more understood. Her water energy, my fire; we see things with clarity, through both sets of eyes. Perfectly balanced, in every possible way. Two lovers, one soul.

What a ride it has been, but little did we know then that we had only just hopped into the railcars. The ride had only just begun.

Chapter Five

My Awakening

I remember the precise time my awakening began. Well, I should say, I remember the time that I associate with my awakening. It was the back end of a confronting week, a beautiful time that I look back on fondly. I had been in Michelle's life for a few months by that stage and things were looking up. With my separation mostly behind me I was starting to look to the future and beginning to reach out for help to better understand subtle but definite changes in my approach to life.

Before I get into this I need to clarify something. I knew very little at this time - I mean, I knew very little of the inner workings of the universe and I honestly had no idea what was next for me. But I did have some understanding of my life. I have always thought of myself as a self-aware person. Although I may not have known how to beat the demons in my life, I did know that they were there.

However, by this stage I had known for some time that my life had been closely watched, guided gently but confidently. I hadn't associated my understanding of this to anything in particular; just a knowledge that I have always fallen on my feet, that everything would be O.K. for me despite my troubled mind. There were some simple rules around this concept. I knew I had to work hard, take action and not be negatively influenced by others. I tried to live a good life and I lived by the motto: "If I give it my absolute best, what happens next was supposed to be and there will be no regrets."

The first stage of my relationship with Michelle was a great dance. The rollercoaster was fun, full of laughter, light and ecstasy-filled. To be honest, life was looking up and my focus was on her. Then it started to change. I started to focus on *me*. It was as if somehow being in her company showed me I was worth loving. I was worth attending to - as if I needed some sort of permission. Her love of me showed me I was worth loving and that I needed to love myself more. This gave me a confidence that I hadn't previously known. I noticed an increased desire for knowledge, a need for clarification to some long unasked questions. I realised that it was time to ask some questions out loud. It was time to take

CHAPTER FIVE

a risk.

I made a bold leap. With my past behind me, my troubles from my teenage years done and dusted, I started to actively seek answers to the many questions I had. It felt good to be curious; it felt great to finally get some answers. With Michelle by my side supporting me through it all, it really was an easier step to make. As often happens with these types of things, one question led to another, and then another. I developed a thirst that was unquenchable - but little did I expect the most profound answer was going to become my greatest teacher.

I started to understand more and faster than I had previously ever been able too, as I sought answers in every facet of my life. Most of the time this led me to more questions, down rabbit holes I would never have thought to look, simply because I never knew they existed. By surrendering to the desire for knowledge I allowed the universe to provide what was needed - avenues for exploration that I didn't think of myself. Some came to dead ends. Others came to multiple forks in the road. Either way, all were beneficial and led me to this point. Nothing was too weird; all was beautiful and provided exactly what I needed, when I needed it. It was a process of self-reflection and universal understanding. What was my place in all this, where did I fit in?

In the search of answers, I sought guidance in a few special souls. The reading and researching helped to clarify a lot for me, but I needed more. I needed guidance. I found this guidance in a couple of knowing souls, one of whom became my spiritual teacher - a knowing soul of similar age, but with a world of experience I longed to understand. I related specifically to this gentleman because of his own struggle with the ego that lies within all of us - a major issue for me and my life experience.

I saw a lot of myself in him (as he apparently did in me), but it was his understanding of the role his ego played in his life, his development and his journey, that resonated with me the most. My work with him opened up a number of doors for me in areas I didn't know were possible, and his gifts were, without doubt, divinely connected.

Through the relationship with my teacher, I developed a curiosity in the possibility of reincarnation, past-life connections to current life experiences. I learned about soul families and the way we reincarnate within soul groups. People from this life are likely to have experienced past lives with you. All playing different roles, seeking different life experiences. This led me to searching through my past lives. Revisiting them in great detail. What I found were extraordinary, heart-pounding memories dating back many thousands of years -cellular-based memories that contained anything I needed to know. I remember some pretty exotic

CHAPTER FIVE

locations, but most of them were very routine, pretty run-of-the-mill; but I didn't care, because it was so exciting to be remembering. I found out who in my current life I had shared past lives with. This realisation to me was profound. Not only do humans reincarnate, but we often do it within soul-based networks. It was fascinating how relationships changed from life to life, but mostly how souls often reincarnated together, in groups, in families. It became apparent to me that we often worked with souls we trusted to help each other learn the lessons we needed to learn; we worked together, through soul-based contracts.

However, one past life left me flawed. Left me speechless and feeling inadequate. I neither expected, nor did I feel worthy at all. It became an overwhelmingly emotional time for me. For days I cried uncontrollably, but the tears were of happiness, a joy that I had never felt before - a joy I, frankly, did not feel worthy of. Not surprising given my issues of worthiness. It was surreal. Very surreal.

This past life regression coincided with a culmination of events coming from all sorts of people. Different people from different walks of life, all unconnected; yet the messages from them were the same. I was apparently here to *teach*. To teach others, lots of others.

FREE FROM FEAR

Now this was a little hard to swallow for me. I brushed most of this off as people just trying to prop me up, just trying to make me feel good. But I did wonder: what would I be teaching anyone about? I hardly had a tough life to learn from. I was hardly awakened, and really didn't feel like anyone would listen anyhow. I mean, come on! Me, a teacher? Yeah right!

So on one of the many drives back to the farm it all unravelled. Like I did many times before, I would call Michelle on the speaker phone to talk through things. We would use this time to debrief, to talk through the many things that crossed my mind on a journey like this. I mentioned to her that my teacher at that time had shared some insight that he had had about me. He told me that I was also here to teach others. If I didn't take his counsel so intimately I would have scoffed at him, also. But he was insistent and I was more confused. I just couldn't see myself teaching. Then clarity arrived.

I asked Michelle why did she think people from different walks of life keep telling me this, and she replied with a very simple, "Andrew, you already are. You have been teaching others for some time now." BAM!!!

It came to me... the flood waters rose, and rose fast. The information flooded my body with unbelievable happiness, divine love of such immense beauty rushed in with the excitement of a

CHAPTER FIVE

child's Christmas morning. I arrived safely at the farm forever a changed man.

I floated around for days. Four days, to be precise. There isn't a drug on this planet that would come close to what I experienced. It was unconditional love direct from the universe - my reward for my willingness to take a bold step. Then I noticed something started to happen: a visualisation appeared before me.

For four days it was like living inside a large sphere. In each area of the sphere there were different jigsaw puzzles. Each one seemed alive, moving like ants going about their work, slowly completing themselves. Then every five minutes or so I would notice a piece here or a piece there, each one representing a moment in my life. There were thousands of pieces, maybe millions, working away feverishly. As surreal as this was I found the entire process peaceful, reassuring. With the amount of love pouring in it was hardly surprising I felt so good, but it was going to be a while before I realised my Angels were doing their very best, once again.

Slowly I floated around the farm for four days, beautifully reliving my life bit by bit. Not in any sensible order - until I noticed that some of the puzzles were complete, without edges, forming slowly with other puzzles. What was this all about? What exactly was happening here? I wasn't terribly concerned, I had no reason to fear anything, I was curious. However I soon realised sometime around day four, that all the puzzles were forming together and creating a big picture of myself. The message was clear. Each piece was not only a point in my life, but a key synchronistic event that was necessary to bring me here. Each and every thing that has happened in my life was happening to ensure I would arrive at this very point. Now.

This may seem like a simple realisation but it was very profound for me. It was a singular point everything funnelled into. Everything - every person, feeling, event, disaster in my life - came to this one infinite point. Now. Even events that happened outside of my own life experience, but were integral to their influence on my life experience, appeared within this visualisation.

But what did this all mean? What was I supposed to do with this information? It took me a few days to debrief before clarity started to flow with relentless abandon.

I had always wondered what brought me to the farm? Why this farm? Why then? Why had no one else bought it in the two years it had been on the market? Was I that big a fool? The hopeless romantic I always knew myself as? Maybe, but I soon began to realise that everything in the Universe is perfect. Everything, no matter how big or small, how good or bad, black or white, or how significant or otherwise. Everything has its place; and when it is in

CHAPTER FIVE

place, it has a purpose - a job to do that nothing else can achieve. Just like humans on this great planet. We all have a unique job to do, a purpose, a calling.

For weeks to come the synchronistic events that I knew as my life experience came flooding through, bit by bit, like jigsaw puzzle pieces. The story was explained in great detail: why I was abused as a fifteen-year-old, why I married, bought a house, saved a puppy from the pound, had children. Why I decided to fix myself in July 2007. The realisations I had that led me to want more space and to look for the farm.

Even the list I wrote of "what the property had to be" was so detailed I thought it would be difficult to find. It stated things like: good rainfall, temperate climate, close enough to the beach but within rolling green hills - even with a mountain at its north-western side. At the time I thought the list was deliberately detailed to make it impossible to find the right property, but then I realised it was, in fact, to exclude all others. You see, everything I ever experienced was divinely mastered to ensure I arrive here, in the Now. My dreams, my visualisations of buildings yet to be built, all became clear. The gardens, the new road, the people - all part of the divine plan.

Even my new partner Michelle had been looking for property in the region for some years before we even knew each other existed. Why there? Why the Tilba region, some three hours away from were each of us unknowingly lived at the time? Was she drawn to the area as well? It appeared so.

I had also realised two key things. One: I was not alone. Ever. Not for one single second. Two: this whole thing was much, much bigger than I realised. So big, in fact, that whatever was orchestrating this master plan was seriously in cahoots with some very powerful beings. Seriously connected.

The realisations continued, and never stopped. The information flowed constantly, sometimes it was overbearing and I learnt to slow it down and sometimes switch it off. It wasn't an ideal method, but one I was comfortable and well-practiced with for many years. Alcohol. A great way to disconnect you from everything. The reason for my need to disconnect was (again) about my issues with worthiness. I am not sure I will truly ever learn that lesson, but I am trying.

The truly blessed realisation for me brings me back to the past life regression I had experienced some weeks before. It was still an emotional thing for me, but my acceptance was different now. I was no longer confused. I no longer felt as inadequate. I no longer felt fear about it.

In my past life - the life that I believe was possibly my first physical world lifetime - was a truly divine life. I was the protector

CHAPTER FIVE

of the land with golden beaches and grand architecture made from a light-coloured stone of massive proportions. Large pyramids were around, as was the Great Crystal Palace. It was my duty to protect and love many people, a lesson that I was going to relearn for many, many lifetimes.

As a guardian of this key land in history, I found myself in love with a mortal woman. A very beautiful woman. Although she was of this world, her beauty transcended universes. The love with this mortal woman was pure, in every way. Divinely inspired, although frowned upon by other less understanding souls. I was very tall, strong and apparently very handsome. She was beautiful in every possible way. The love we felt was direct from heaven and could not be corrupted in any way. The guilt I was to carry for many lifetimes was as much about her as it was about the people.

I struggled with the concept of being this Great Guardian in a past life. My teacher at the time told me not to get too caught up in this, as we have all played great roles in the past, of one sort or another. In fact, he was quick to point out that we have all played terrible roles in the past too.

But I couldn't deal with the idea of being this Great Guardian. I wasn't worthy of that title, that role. But in the months to come it all fell into place. Not only was I a guardian, but I was a Great Guardian, tall and powerful. Remembered for centuries. Strong of heart and pure in my purpose. I have carried through many gifts from this role, but also much heartache. The guilt I felt from failing in my duty to protect the thousands under my watch, when the city fell during the great floods, carried on with me over many, many lifetimes. The great city was destined to fall and was never seen again. It was erased from humanity's records, never to be fully understood. This guilt and my guardian role was portrayed across many past life regressions (some human and some not) but it all made sense now. It is a lesson I am still to learn. It is a key thing I need to let go of. I must surrender this guilt and allow for the peace to return.

Coming to terms with the fact that I was once this Great Guardian helped me understand why I was chosen for the role I have in this life. The clarity flowed, my mind was now open, and the information and messaging became clearer each and every day.

I had been brought to this point to create something truly wonderful. Brought to a place of ancient wisdom, of great spiritual significance to hundreds or thousands of generations before me. As it turns out, I am not alone in this as my Angels had been in cahoots with the universe all along.

Then it dawned on me... Oh my dearest God, thank you for this great honour you have bestowed upon me. God, I hope I don't mess it up.

Chapter Six

From Clarity Came Consciousness

The next period of my life came thick and fast. Questions filled my mind and I flooded my brain with as much information I could get my hands on. I read book after book, consuming ideals, concepts and teachings from many great teachers, both past and present. Concepts that would have been impossible to grasp became easy to understand and the universal truth became a language that I felt strangely comfortable with. Although I had started questioning everything in life some years before, the clarity that I had now was just delicious - almost limitless. I started to enjoy living in a way I would never have believed.

Michelle had always been a person in search of the truth, the answers to the big questions. She had travelled many paths trying to find the answers. Michelle's understanding of religious texts of various beliefs was enormously helpful to me. I could bounce ideas off her and she became a great sounding board for my thoughts as we played them out together.

She introduced me to Eckhart Tolle and his incredibly gentle way of explaining the need for *presence* in our life: what this means and how we can achieve it in our own lives. His concept of the ego, conscious and unconscious living was very profound for me and I accepted it as my own truth. I related deeply with his teachings and developed a thirst for more.

I read books when I had time and listened to audiobooks when I travelled. The idea of being able to listen quickly caught on for me, as I could take it anywhere. The world of podcasts opened up opinions that would not have otherwise been available to me, as did the growing number of spiritual connections I made through attending seminars and weekend events.

Then something rather strange started to happen. People started showing up. Random people started appearing in my life. Showing up at the farm after being *told* to come. By whom or what

CHAPTER SIX

I don't know. These people were incredibly spiritual people, spiritual teachers, shamans, and psychics. I don't say this to enhance my own ego, or to impress you, but merely to impress upon you, that when you are connected you are more inclined to listen to your inner voice, your inspiration - even when it tells you to jump in your car and drive for eight hours until you are told to pull over and get out (as a number of people did). When you are connected you are more inclined to attract and listen to the messages the universe sends you - the opportunities the universe provides for you to create the life you choose to experience. The unconscious people in the world would just call this crazy, spiritual mumbo jumbo, because they choose not to understand it. But it is real. Very, very real.

I soon learned to realise these people were bringing clear, synchronistic messages from the universe. They were mostly brought to my doorstep to reinforce a message I needed to hear, or to remind me that I was on track, or simply that what I was already doing was working and they could see it too. Soon, nothing became too weird, too "out there" for me to handle. Even the arrival of unique spirits to help the animals on my farm give birth to their babies wasn't enough to phase me. My world had opened up to experiences of psychic surgery, remote healing and clairvoyance well beyond anything I could have ever expected or even started to understand. All of these people were very gifted people, and the work they do is divinely influenced through good hearts and a need to help humanity evolve.

It was about this time that I noticed that the Wise Old Man was a little cleverer than I had previously given him credit for. I thought that he was just some wildly romantic poet from centuries ago that was using my fingers to type emails or poems to ensure that Michelle and I were not going to mess up what needed to be. I wrote many an email, but also many poems that carried his unique writing style. Yet, rereading them some time later, Michelle and I realised one very unique aspect to them we hadn't previously appreciated. They weren't only amazing poems, but they were prophetic messages that have since come true.

In fact, of the three or four key poems that we had articulated as being "directly" from him (as opposed to poems that I had written deliberately to try and copy his style, which were nowhere near as good) we realised that, on that date that we read them, we were currently halfway through one of the middle poems. The beginning of the poem had recently happened, despite it being written some many months or years beforehand.

I also had these poems independently verified from some highly trusted spiritual leaders to ensure that my ego wasn't creating some false truth. This verification took time for me to

CHAPTER SIX

accept. It wasn't about anything but my self-worth, my worthiness to be chosen; but of course, that was also my ego, because I wasn't chosen - I am just a channel to enable a necessary outcome to be realised.

Now please understand why I am sharing all this with you. This is not a tale of how lucky I am, or how special I am, but more proof of a number of interesting ideas that I believe to be true. Although I am now aware that I am a divine spiritual being having a human experience, I am in no way different to you. The awakening is available to all of us, and it is very achievable. My story only seeks to highlight the changes that can happen as a result of this type of journey. It is the journey of a very normal, everyday person.

Now, please keep in mind that everyone's journey is different, as each of us have different purposes, lessons and teachings to fulfil. But making the choice to seek the answers is, in itself, the first step that everyone can make.

It doesn't matter how busy you are, how rich you are, what your relationship status is or how many friends you have on Facebook. You are here on this planet for a reason. I am here to tell you: that reason, and the truth of that reason, is not as far out of reach as you may think. In fact it is surprisingly simple.

Ultimately it comes down to *choices*. Simple choices.

FREE FROM FEAR

Once I had realised what my awakening was, I started a process of understanding, which in turn provided clarity. It was this clarity that enabled my conscious state to be recognised, or more importantly, to recognise when my unconscious state was taking over so that I could counter that with decisions enabling consciousness.

Got that?

No? Neither did I at first.

This is where the reading helped. People, many people, many great teachers, have written many great books. Modern teachers of the truth are the Eckhart Tolles, Deepak Chopras and Wayne Dyers of the world. What they enable, through their own experiences, is the right words (and each one will appeal differently to different people) to enable us to understand what is happening or what is possible for each and every one of us. They will say, just as I say, that none of us are special in our teachings. We aren't discovering anything new.

All we are doing is trying to enable people to remember their own truth.

All we are doing is realising the ancient knowledge that is passed through us to you and adapting it using a modern language or context.

All we are doing is remembering what we are here to

CHAPTER SIX

remember. I cannot tell you what you are here to remember, because it is different for each and every one of us. However, what I can offer you is some steps towards the path of identifying your state of mind, to enable you to choose consciousness over unconsciousness. That will hopefully enable you to connect with your inspiration to start the process towards understanding.

It is through understanding that we grow. Through this growth we can learn to connect, and through this connection we can begin to understand.

Let's break down what this is all about. Let's start to understand the ultimate dichotomy, how it influences our truth and what that ultimately means in the way we feel, act and listen. I believe that by understanding our feelings we can learn to listen to what is being said with the purpose of understanding why we are here, so we can start to fulfil that purpose.

Chapter Seven

Love and Fear

Most contemporary spiritual teachers say our relationship to everything in the universe is purely based on one of two things. Those two key things construct every thought, every feeling and/or every emotion we will ever experience. No matter what you do, how you feel, communicate or relate to others, everything relates to one of two things.

Love or Fear.

This dichotomy is the ultimate dichotomy. They are not just opposites, but the ultimate opposites. The universe is full of them, and they are necessary for each other to exist. One cannot exist without the other, with one simple exception: God. Because God is the only thing that is both.

FREE FROM FEAR

There is hot and cold, up and down, tall and short, big and small; and of course, light and dark. There are opposites to everything. But all opposites are dependent on perspective. They can all be different for different people, because all carry different perspectives based on what they see, feel and interpret.

The emotional sphere is certainly no different. There is happy and sad, calm and angry, pride and shame, innocence and guilt; and of course, pleasure and pain. All of these things, everything we feel, think and emotionally relate to, comes from one of two root causes: Love or Fear.

Now, when I grew up I was taught that the opposite of Love was hate. But hate is merely a construct of Fear; as such, cannot be a root cause. So it is with anger, shame and guilt. The root cause of all these is Fear. Fear constructs everything in the absence of Love; and in fact, Fear is the cause of everything that isn't created by Love.

This is an important fact to understand because what this all relates to is how we perceive things and how we relate to what is happening around us. Have we based our thoughts or feelings, our perception of what we are experiencing, on Love or Fear? These two factors provide the filter through which we see our immediate environment and influences our responses to anything and everything we experience. This knowledge is not only paramount

CHAPTER SEVEN

to our understanding of all things we experience, it is also the way we relate to our immediate environment and is vital to the process we use to deconstruct our response to anything and everything we experience.

So let me break it down for you. Every thought, every emotion, and every decision we have made and will ever make, is based on Love or Fear. The consequence of every thought we think, every emotion we feel, and decision we make is also influenced by either Love or Fear. This is ultimately determined by perspective. If you choose Love as a basis of your thought, emotion or decision then the outcome and the consequence will also be based on Love. Alternatively, if you choose Fear (consciously or unconsciously) as the basis of your thought, emotion or decision then the consequence will also be based on Fear. What I am here to show you is that you can control the outcomes that the universe presents, purely by your intentions, statements and actions. This is where free will comes in. It is all about choice.

I believe we would all agree that Love creates a happy, joyful experience. It conjures images of beauty and good times. Fear, on the other hand, immediately creates darkness in your mind - it shuts you down and disempowers you from moving in a positive direction. What if I told you that you can rid yourself of Fear and remove it altogether from being a controlling factor in your life?

FREE FROM FEAR

Sound too good to be true? It really isn't.

What if I pointed out to you that Fear is not only unnecessary, but can be switched on and off like a television? I know, you think I'm either crazy or brilliant, it's got to be one of the two; but let me explain by first understanding what we are dealing with.

Love is the most powerful force in the universe. There is no argument to be had with that. Love creates life; it expands, grows and multiplies in a massive way. Nature uses Love on a grand scale, each and every day. Love creates grand things, and can overcome all obstacles, no matter how difficult or challenging they may be. Love is divine - and I don't mean wonderful, delicious or incredible (although it is also all those things). It is provided directly from your higher self - so directly, so immediately, that it instantly transcends all space and time. It travels far and wide across all corners of the infinite cosmos in an instant. It is omnipresent, or in other words, it is in all places, at all times, in all ways. Pure, unconditional, Love.

Love creates friends with strong bonds and encourages success in others. Love is selfless and asks for nothing in return. Love offers freedom and delivers divine inspiration. Love creates a thirst for knowledge and shares knowledge through applied constructs like Wisdom. Love is everything you need - so much so, that when you accept it into your life, you will never be left

CHAPTER SEVEN

wanting. Love is as amazing, remarkable and incredible as it gets. It is here on this planet; it is real. It is not just something that is in heaven. It is on earth as it is in heaven. Love is everywhere, in everything. It is offered and accepted in all living creatures, plants, animals and beings. Love, simply put, is as delicious as it could possibly get.

All ancient texts talk about love - The Quran, the Bhagavad-Gita, the Talmud and the Bible to name a few – as do many modern and not-so-modern texts. It is a universal language, across all beings, universe-wide. First Corinthians 13 speaks of it as my truth:

"If I speak in the tongues of men or of angels, but do not have love, I am only a resounding gong or a clanging cymbal. If I have the gift of prophecy and can fathom all mysteries and all knowledge, and if I have a faith that can move mountains, but do not have love, I am nothing. If I give all I possess to the poor and give over my body to hardship that I may boast, but do not have love, I gain nothing.

"Love is patient, love is kind. It does not envy, it does not boast, it is not proud. It does not dishonour others, it is not self-seeking, it is not easily angered, it keeps no record of wrongs. Love does not delight in evil but rejoices with the truth. It always protects, always trusts, always hopes, always perseveres.

"Love never fails. But where there are prophecies, they will

cease, where there are tongues, they will be stilled; where there is knowledge, it will pass away. For we know in part and we prophesy in part, but when completeness comes, what is in part disappears. When I was a child, I talked like a child, I thought like a child, I reasoned like a child. When I become a man, I put the ways of childhood behind me. For now we see only a reflection as in a mirror; then we shall see face to face. Now I know in part; then I shall know fully, even as I am fully known.

"And now these three remain: faith, hope and love. But the greatest of these is love."

Fear, on the other hand, confines, damages and destroys. Fear is the ego's master. It is controlling, damning and poisonous. Its darkness can also reach all areas of the cosmos, and it wants to spread like a disease of the mind. It can be caught and passed from one party to another. It is used by governments and religions the world over to control its people. Corporations use it as a tool to generate profits. It destroys the body, the earth and the lifeblood of the universe. It only wants to corrupt, as Fear only desires pain and suffering. Fear creates drama, problems, and directly influences your health in a negative way. Fear allows disease through the accumulations of stress, acids and toxins in your body that enables disease to take hold. Fear is said to be the by-product of free choice, the original sin, the corruptor of the creation.

CHAPTER SEVEN

But the great secret no one wants you to know is that Fear has no strength. Fear is weak and easily overcome. Fear is the schoolyard bully, a coward with no confidence.

Despite wielding so much power, despite appearing so strong, Fear is also weak and it has no friends despite needing them to survive. Fear is a corruption of the mind but will never create anything. Fear is its own destructive force; it is its own kryptonite. Fear cannot stand up to Love. They cannot be friends together, because Fear is scared of Love despite the fact that Love truly loves Fear. Fear fights Love hard and dirty, yet Love embraces Fear with nothing but Love. Why? Because Love is unconditional, non-judgemental and unwavering. Love accepts all things for what they are and for what they offer. Love knows that all it can do is offer itself, sacrifice itself for the greater good. Love is the ultimate hero.

Fear cannot survive in the presence of Love, just as darkness cannot survive the presence of light. The mere existence of Love dispels all fear. ALL FEAR.

But the big question sitting in the back of your mind is probably, "What does this have to do with me? I don't feel fear, I don't let fear run my life."

Now I would ask in the first instance, "What is fear to you?" Do you understand how fear presents, or shows up, in your life? It is often misinterpreted, ignored or misunderstood. The vast majority of individuals experience fear on a daily, if not an hourly basis; but rarely is it ever recognised for what it is. In fact, it has become such an integral part of everyone's daily routine that most people don't have a chance of recognising it - even if they wanted to.

With the rising instances of anxiety, depression and illness within the modern world I would like to suggest that it is possible that fear *is* a player in your life. The good news is that it doesn't have to be. You can decide that fear is no longer welcome in your life. But first you need to be able to identify it, understand where it presents in your life, and then make the right choices to eliminate it.

Fear often presents in many different forms to many different people. Fear can arise in a person who is anxious by nature. Or, someone who likes drama in their life and attaches their self-importance to the drama and their resolution of it. Anxiety can be crippling for some people, particularly those with a "disease to please" and those who are afraid of conflict. Fear is used in all aspects of the media to entertain, control and sell. It is used by governments to control its constituents; and of course, even religions use fear: to keep people in the pews, to keep them paying money, and to keep them conforming. They even created the concept of the Devil and Hell as a controlling tool to keep people

CHAPTER SEVEN

coming in to confess their sins. In fact, the whole process of confessing your sins is to repeatedly remind you to realise your own failings, enable the ego to put you down, and force people to repent and feel guilt and shame. Even the idea of God being separate is a deliberate process to disconnect you from your own abundant potential. You are told to confess *to* God, to pray *to* God. Why? God is within you, you are a part of God. Like the trees, and creatures and Mother Nature. A priest has no more connection to God than the so-called sinner does.

However, it doesn't really matter how fear presents in your life; what is ultimately important is how you allow fear to present - to what degree you allow fear in, and how often you allow fear to consume or control you.

But you say, "I have no control over the anxiety I feel. I cannot control feeling scared when conflict presents itself in my life." What if I said you *do* have control? In fact, you can control every one of your emotional states. You can control when you are happy, or sad, or scared, or anxious. All of it is within your control because all of it is of your making. The trick is learning to recognise and resolve what you *don't* want in your emotional state, and activate what you *do* want.

I hear you say, "But we need fear in our life to stop us from burning our hand on a hot plate, or to stop us from walking into danger." But that isn't entirely true. The physical response caused by the neurological effects of burning skins cells that alerts your nervous systems to the feeling of pain is enough to remove your hand from the cause; that is not what we are talking about here. Fear doesn't stop you from doing that again and again; it is the desire to not relive the physical neurological pain caused by the event that stops you. I also believe that what stops you from walking into danger *is* your instinct, which is a construct of Love, delivered through inspiration, which is enabled through a state of presence, either unconsciously or consciously - but certainly not Fear. We need to understand that the egoic, Fear-run story of disconnection is different to the gentle words of inspiration. They feel different, and that is the key.

When God released the concept of free will on the earth, God made everything we experience in our individual existence a product of our choices. Ultimately, Fear is what is present in the absence of Love. That is, when we choose to live without Love, Fear naturally fills the void. So these choices result in constructs of Fear that arise from the "mind chatter" that occurs as a result of a loss of presence. Learning to recognise fear, and to resolve the constructs that come as a result of its presence, is the key to overcoming the battle of the ego. The ego is Fear's greatest ally; the ego keeps us in our Fear-controlled world and inhibits our ability

CHAPTER SEVEN

to choose Love.

I believe that all anxiety and depression is, at its core, a feeling of disconnection - a feeling of the absence of Love in our lives. We feel like we have no support in our lives, no friends to help when we need it, no one who loves us unconditionally. When we are young, most of us are fortunate to know that our parents love us unconditionally. We know we are safe, looked after, and have a roof over our head. But when we have thoughts that we are on our own, our perspective changes to Fear- based constructs and the ego is now in full force. At that point, the ego has full control.

It doesn't have to be that way.

Ultimately, Fear is a construct of the physical world; therefore, it can be unmade, controlled or (better still) resolved, for good. As humans we are very powerful spiritual beings. In fact, in comparison to the construct of the world we have been taught and conditioned to believe in, we have powers well beyond the superpowers of our comic book makers' creations. We are limited not by our physical world, but by the physical world we believe in. This belief has only developed through what you are taught: by your families, your peers, your governments and your education systems. You can change your beliefs at any time - you just have to choose to do so by recognising which beliefs are not working for you, and by deciding to allow new beliefs that enable you to live

FREE FROM FEAR

the way you wish to live.

We need to understand that Fear is just a construct of your upbringing. Since its existence is created by the belief structure created by your upbringing, its power is limited to the very same belief structures created by your upbringing. The key is to change the belief structures that no longer serve you, open your heart, and allow your heart to retrain your mind. You have to open your mind up to the possibilities that are well beyond the limitations you currently have in place. When this is accomplished, unmetered freedom is possible. That not only means freedom from Fear, but freedom from all the learned constructs that your belief system was built upon, which led to the unhealthy parts of your life.

You need to know that the heart is pure, as the heart only works with Love, and Love is pure, as it is the only language used by God. God uses Love to communicate with all of us. We are not only God's children; we are also a part of God, as are all of the animals, the plants, the planets and the universe. God is (as you are) a being of Love and light. But Fear is a physical-world construct. Fear is taught at a very early age, consciously or unconsciously. Babies are not born into fear; they are born into love, and it is their physical world realization that develops into Fear. Some learn it faster than others, but it is learned by all. All

CHAPTER SEVEN

emotions, feelings, and behaviours that stem from Fear are also learned; they are a part of our physical world journey, and partly the reason why we are here: to experience in the physical world what we cannot experience in the spiritual world. They are partly the reason why you choose to reincarnate back into a physical world, because Fear is not something you can experience in the spiritual world or in heaven. It is only a concept that can be understood from your physical experience.

"I must say a word about fear. It is life's only true opponent. Only fear can defeat life. It is a clever, treacherous adversary, how well I know. It has no decency, respects no law or convention, shows no mercy. It goes for your weakest spot, which it finds with unnerving ease. It begins in your mind always... so you must fight hard to express it. You must fight hard to shine the light of words upon it. Because if you don't, if your fear becomes a wordless darkness that you avoid, perhaps even manage to forget, you open yourself to further attacks of fear because you never truly fought the opponent who defeated you." *

So let's break this down further. If you are a spiritual being

---

* Martel, Yann. *Life of Pi*. New York: Harcourt, Inc., 2001.

FREE FROM FEAR

choosing to live a human experience, and all that it has to offer (including fear and fear-based emotions and behaviours), don't you think that you can also choose *not* to experience them? If in your truest state you are a being of light, and Love is all you need (is, in fact all you are) and Fear is secondary to Love in all instances, then surely Love can conquer Fear. Let's break this down further again and delve even deeper.

I want to explain that I use the word *God* to refer to the supreme universal power that is referred to in all belief systems, irrespective of what your religion may use as a label. I in no way mean to assert that any one religion is right or wrong, or any better than any others, in the use of the label "God." *God* was a term I was raised with, and also, a term I fought against for many years. I use the term *God* as a universal label to describe the ultimate creator, the ultimate universal energy that is everything. The Source, Allah, Krishna, The Creator, just to name a few.

God is all-powerful. God created everything. God is everything that is and everything that isn't because God created everything, IS everything. Now these are some pretty big statements, and there are many books and texts covering them, so I won't break them down further here; but accepting that fundamental truth is the starting point.

So, that means that because everything that *is*, is God, then

CHAPTER SEVEN

everything that *is*, is also Love. Therefore, as God is Love, and You are God, then You are Love. I will let that sit with you for a moment.

Next, we need to understand that we have chosen an existence in a physical dimension to experience all we can. Within that dimension there are factors at play that don't exist in the spiritual realm. Surely then, these dimensional factors are secondary - not primary, as we are told to believe. If we are spiritual beings at our core, and our home is Heaven (for want of a better word), then surely everything we experience here on Earth is secondary. It feels primary - we are taught that it is primary, but it is in fact secondary. Surely then, what is primary has ultimate strength. This is Love.

So let's get back to Earth for a moment. You enter this life to learn matters of the physical world and to experience everything it has to offer. When you leave this life you cannot take anything from this physical world with you, including all matters associated to the physical world. All you leave with is what is in your heart - your soul. Things like memories and experiences from this life. As the soul is a direct part of God and God is Love, all you can leave with is Love. So material things – money, and all physical things; in fact, and all other matters stemming from anything other than Love - cannot leave with you either. Constructs of the physical world stay, and memories and experiences carry on with you to your next journey. You leave your ego behind.

To clarify: I don't mean that physical things are made of Fear, or that the physical world is made of Fear. They aren't. They are made of however you perceive them. Remember, God is everything, and God is Love; therefore, everything is Love. What creates Fear, what enables it to exist, is our thoughts of it. Our thoughts of Fear. If you approach the physical with Love in your heart then the physical radiates Love. If you feel Fear, then the physical radiates Fear. Love and Fear are not defined by physical or non-physical; in the physical plane they are constructs of the heart and the mind. In the physical plane (and in your experience of that physical plane) you receive the added benefit of being able to experience the physical, which you cannot experience in the spiritual plane. What comes with that experience is the option of being able to experience Fear. Although not a physical characteristic, it is part of your experience of the physical plane. Fear is created by the mind, not the heart.

All things that aren't derived from Love are derived from Fear. Fear creates anger, guilt, shame, disappointment and judgement. The tool Fear uses to implement these control mechanisms is the ego. The ego rules the unconscious mind with these mechanisms on a daily basis. It is less prevalent in the

CHAPTER SEVEN

mornings because during your sleep, it is widely believed that your soul travels across the cosmos to play with all your friends and allow your soul a break from the ego-controlled physical world you chose to live in. In fact, your soul needs a break from the pressures of the physical world's fear- based constructs. As your day progresses, living in the physical space allows the ego time to take back control. We rarely wake up with our ego in full swing, although for some people it is possible. This takes time each day.

As the conscious mind slowly becomes aware of the ego and the games it plays on a daily basis it starts to unravel the puzzle that has been developed by education in the physical world. The heart plays a role in waking up the conscious state, because the heart is only interested in Love prevailing. The heart knows that Love is all there is. The heart can only speak the truth, and it cannot lie.

But the ego doesn't give up easily. The ego has the edge in the human mind. That's because the human (depending on age, environment and upbringing) often has its only friend in the ego. The ego needs the human to stay in the unconscious state to maintain control, to even exist. As a construct of the mind, the ego must make sure it remains a major player, and doesn't want to be known or recognised, because it knows, each time it is recognised for the fear that it portrays, it leaves itself exposed.

FREE FROM FEAR

This is true in the analogy that darkness fears the light, because it knows that it is defenceless against the light. The dark cannot survive in the light. In recognizing the ego, you cast light on its undesirable ways; you show the ego up for what it is, and it often turns in on itself and hides away for another day.

I wish I could say that the ego can be beaten in the physical world, but it cannot – well, not easily. Few mortal beings have ever lived without an ego, and they have become great prophets of Love and Love's mission. The rest of us on the planet maintain an ego and like a virus. The ego is only interested in controlling us. The ego's objective is complete domination, to the point that control results in unconscious living and disconnection from all that is around us. It is the ego's job to separate you from Love to enable Fear to reign. The ego knows we are all connected as one, and therefore it must disconnect us, because it cannot survive whilst we remain connected. Once we are disconnected, the ego can rule through fear and destruction of your ability to connect again.

When I started to understand this I realised that it was no wonder that my awakening happened partly as a result of my own journey, but definitely accelerated as a result of meeting Michelle. When unconditional love is at play in such overwhelmingly large quantities, the ego cannot fight that fight. Because it is made of fear, it can only survive in a fear-based environment. Offering it

CHAPTER SEVEN

love dissolves it.

Fear destroys, Fear weakens, and Fear eventually collapses. When Love is at play, Fear cannot survive, like darkness cannot survive the introduction of light.

The same process is happening for Michelle. Her fear is falling away with the pure, unconditional love that I show her on a daily basis. As fear falls away, she (like all others) gains strength and finds her own love; and that builds and builds until consciousness reigns. Then, once consciousness is realised and recognised, and the tools are learned and understood to enable regular recognition, the rest is history.

Now, this is not a given. We can retract to our old ways easily. But through steady practice, healthy living, looking after ourselves and helping others, we can be well on our way to solidifying a permanent and unshakable structure of Love in our lives.

I remember the day that Fear left my existence for good. Since then I have experienced things that are merely constructs of what my ego remembers as Fear, and it has tried to draw me back into them in an effort to rebuild a control mechanism over me. But it hasn't worked. I am more and more aware of my ego every day, and you can be, too. I will show you throughout this book how to recognise your ego for what it is, and understand its ways, so you can see what it produces in your life. Through this process you will

FREE FROM FEAR

start to understand that by choosing Love in your life, you will not only dispel Fear, but you will manifest all that Love has to offer. You will start to win that battle - but it is not a battle you ever want to leave unguarded, because the ego is a crafty beast, cunning and devious. However, through your awareness, and by calling it to account and offering it Love, you can dispel it and send it packing.

I believe the reason why we reincarnate into this physical existence is to learn to overcome the power of the ego and to choose Love. I believe this is ultimately why we are here. I believe we come here to seek (and to help others to seek) the joy that comes from acknowledging the ego, and knowing that it is all about the choice we have as beings: to choose Love over the ego.

We came here to experience everything the physical plane has to offer. However, that doesn't mean we have to suffer as a result of it. It doesn't mean we have to be ruled by Fear, or its friend the ego, and their poisonous ways. Our life, and how we live it, is our choice. We are the only being in the entire universe that can create our life's experience. We can choose how we want our life to play out and how we want the universe to respond through our life experience. We can choose a life of Love or Fear.

I choose Love, because it is what I am

Chapter Eight

The Ego and Its Influence Over You

The Ego is a magnificent construct, developed over many lifetimes throughout mankind's journey. The Ego arose from the time on our planet that is referenced by the Adam and Eve story, the time of "Original Sin" as the Church calls it. This story is used to describe how God created "free will" when God gave us a choice to experience Love or Fear with all they have to offer. It was at this point that the Ego became a tool of Fear. Fear developed the Ego and figured out through its development how to manipulate, control and master it's host: You.

In fact, the story of Adam and Eve gives us the best analogy of the Ego and how it presents in your life. The Ego is represented by the snake: that controlling, manipulative, crafty voice in your head that seeks to get you to believe in everything that is wrong in others *around* you and everything that is wrong *in* you.

The Ego's role is to keep you unconscious - to disconnect you from Source and all that is glorious about the universe. The Ego knows it must do this because the Ego knows the truth: that you are connected, as *One*, to all living beings. The Ego knows that you are connected to all creatures, plants and people. The only way it can survive in the presence of such unconditional love and conscious connection is to disconnect you and separate you from that divine connection by creating stories based on fear and hatred. The Ego is a construct of Fear; the mind is a doorway that Fear uses to enable the Ego to communicate with your thought processes. Most people cannot differentiate between their thoughts and their own divine intuition. In fact, most people are not even aware that divine guidance even exists in their lives, because they have been taught that they *are* the thoughts inside their head and that they are not worthy to hear God's words directly - that is only for the Church's leaders to hear. This couldn't be farther from the truth.

You are not the thoughts in your head. You are, in fact, the calm awareness behind the noise that infiltrates our mind on a

CHAPTER EIGHT

moment-by-moment basis. You are the soul that sits quietly - all loving - awaiting a moment of peace and quiet to whisper gently through the noise. Not the thoughts, but the calm awareness listening to the thoughts, created by the mind. In the same way that you are not your body, because your body is simply a vessel that enables physicality in this world. The mind and the body stays behind upon what we label as "death."

When your body dies, what lies in your heart is what stays with you. Your body, its physical state and the mechanisms that operate it, stay behind on Earth at the end of this life's journey. Your Soul resides within your heart and is your life source; in fact, you are your soul. It is where everything pure emanates from, and it is where your inspiration comes through. Your body and your mind, both physical-world constructs, stay behind. We can understand this better if we look at how we hear different communications.

We need to understand and learn the difference between the voice in our head, what we hear in the physical world, and the inspiration that is available to all of us. We are all taught throughout our childhood that our ears hear everything, so that is why we associate everything in our head to hearing. It's a natural thing for us to do. This, in fact, has nothing to do with the middle ear; it is just picking up background noise. It is about what we are perceiving, which is based on our belief systems. Doctors will tell us that the ear picks up physical world vibrations that is interpreted as sound. Which is true. But physical world vibrations are not the only thing we hear. We also hear a voice in our head, which we call our "thoughts." We believe they come from us - from what we are - and we associate ourselves to them. Deaf people hear the voice in their head and the inspiration in their heart, even if their ears don't work in the same way most of ours do. The voice in our head has nothing to do with our ears.

The voice in our head, is heard by us (mostly unconsciously) but not in the same way the ear hears noise. The mind is creating the voice in our head. Like in the same way we associate ourselves to our body, we also associate ourselves to our mind and our mind's thoughts. We are in fact neither. We are in fact the calm awareness listening to the thoughts.

Most spiritually-connected people will say that our inspiration, our divine connection to all that is, comes through our heart. We may hear it in our head, because our lifetime-generated belief system says that we hear in our head. Our divine inspiration is actually heard through every cell of our body - every single one. Connected through the heart, but heard by our entire system, both physical and metaphysical. There is a big difference between the two. This is just an example to help us understand, what it is that

CHAPTER EIGHT

we are.

Sometimes we need to separate out what we have been taught from what is the truth. Rarely have our leaders in the developed Western world on Earth ever told the truth in the last 3,000 years. They believe that humans are stupid and not capable of understanding the truth. Well, they are wrong - because the truth is coming out and people are waking up.

When your body dies, you - your soul - stays with you, because you are your Soul; your Life Source. Your thoughts and memories of this life travel not far at all, but into another dimensional layer, where Heaven (as some may call it) resides. There you will understand all things, across all dimensions, across all lifetimes, and across all souls, in an instant - and it will all become clear. You will understand that in reality, Love *is* all there is, and Fear doesn't exist, as it is only a construct of the mind - part of the process of being physical in a physical dimension.

I say, why wait till you die to understand this fact, when understanding it now can free you from the pain and the suffering you experience in this life?

Now, I need to be clear about something. It is important to always stay in the present. Many books have been written about this. Eckhart Tolle's *The Power of Now* is one of the best modern texts I have come across. It explains that there is only ever one moment in your life that is in the Now. The past is a memory; the future is a construct of Fear or Love that is based on those past memories. But each moment - each event, act or memorable experience - is all happening in the Now. The Now is eternal, infinite, and the mere pinpoint of right now, where you experience everything. Spiritual leaders for centuries have proven that staying in the present moment not only clears your mind, but also opens up yourself and your lifetime experience to the wonders of the universe. It opens doors, creates successes and provides abundance like no other. Staying present is one of the most powerful tools we have. But it isn't without its difficulties.

Staying present is important because it is through being present that our connection is strongest, and therefore, your ultimate limitless abundance is at its strongest when you stay present. This is delivered through your connection to the one true loving Source, where Love not only conquers all, but where Love manifests greatness in our lives, where it makes physical our deepest desires, and where our thoughts become a reality. In understanding this, you will understand why it is so important to ensure we are having thoughts of Love and not of Fear. But I will touch on that in more detail later.

The Ego will present in many different forms. As Ego is a construct of Fear, the Ego knows that all other constructs of Fear

CHAPTER EIGHT

(like guilt, shame, hate, anger, disappointment and loneliness) are easy and effective strings to pull in order to drag you back under; so, it will use whatever it can to disconnect you. The ego communicates to you through your mind.

Neale Donald Walsch's book, *Conversations with God*,[*] stated, "Mine is always your Highest Thought, your Clearest Word, your Grandest Feeling. Anything less is from another source." What God was saying here is that the heart (that God works through) can only have thoughts of the highest vibration; only thoughts that align with constructs of Love. Any other thought is a construct of Fear used by the Ego to gain control of you again and pull you from your state of Presence - to disconnect you from all that is possible.

Time and time again over the last few months I have been saying to myself, "Go away Ego: I want nothing of your thoughts." This is a good approach for when I catch myself in a spiral of negative thoughts or feelings of ill will towards another. These thoughts can be any thought: the painfully slow drivers in the traffic; aggression towards those interrupting or invading your personal space; frustrations over money; machines breaking down; or, anything that is not happening exactly the way you want

---

[*] Walsch, N. (1996). *Conversations with God: an uncommon dialogue*. New York: G.P. Putnam's Sons.

it to.

So in breaking this all down, I was thinking about the fact that God is all: everything that is and everything that is not. Therefore, God created both the good and the bad. The question then arose: "Why aren't the negative thoughts I have in my head from God, if God is the Alpha and the Omega?"

Well, technically they are. They exist because of God, but they are not from God. They are from my fear-based egoic responses. They are of the physical world created by God, not communication from God. They are created within our own minds.

The premise is that in my true state of Presence, my connection is not only strong and pure, but in fact, only thoughts of the highest vibrational state will come through. As soon as my thoughts change frequency, I have stepped out of my present state and created an avenue for the Ego to return. God doesn't need to have any thoughts, or communicate any thoughts other than ones of the highest vibration. God knows that Love is all there is and all there needs to be. God doesn't need fear-based constructs to be the all-powerful God that God is. God is *not* judgemental and does not punish. God only loves.

So, putting it simply, the easy way to recognise the Ego is to recognise the thought that is not of Love, the thought that is not from a state of presence but from anything other than loving in

CHAPTER EIGHT

nature. Another way is to recognise whenever you are feeling anything other than peace and happiness. Any negative feeling allows the Ego to be present, and the Ego cannot be present when you are connected or experiencing feelings of love, peace or happiness, or for that matter, any feeling derived from any love construct. The Ego cannot be present in a love-driven state, but only in a fear-driven state. When you realise this you should be guided back into the Present, enabling you to denounce the Ego with its fear-based ways and release your mind of the thought patterns you no longer want. You can now focus on the present state, therefore bringing about thought patterns you do want.

If your thoughts are being particularly persistent, and changing your present state seems particularly hard, try changing what you are doing, your location, or the environmental aspects that could be contributing to your downward spiral. Change your state. It is not external things that cause the negative flow; it is always your mind that causes disconnection from the present. Even so, this process can be effective, because the simple act of changing your location, your environment, or what you are doing is an effective way of changing the state you are in, which interrupts your downward thought process.

One master of this technique is Tony Robbins. Tony says that even being silly in times of feeling down immediately reverses our state of mind and snaps us out of our negative pain-based consciousness. He uses examples of jumping up and down and clapping our hands, making loud silly noises and perhaps even getting others to join in. These are all very real and valuable tools that can help us out of a negative state and focus our energy towards positive, love-based thoughts or feelings.

One technique I have unconsciously performed that falls into this category is grabbing my hedge trimmers or secateurs and disappearing into my garden for peace and quiet. This has been a great practice that I now recognise has worked for me over the last 25 years.

Another very simple technique you can use to break a pattern of negative egoic thought processes something I refer to as: **Recognise, Reflect and Resolve.**

1. *Recognise* what is happening to you that you dislike, and recognise the need to change your state of mind.

2. *Reflect* on what you choose to experience in your life. Acknowledge that your negative thoughts are not constructive to your greater good and literally call out the Ego and tell it that you no longer want its negative fear-based ways in your life.

CHAPTER EIGHT

3. *Resolve* to change your thought process to that of a positive one, and take the actions necessary to change your current state.

To make this approach even more effective, you can add to the technique of Recognising the need to change your mind by physically removing yourself from the environmental influences that are contributing to it, or changing the environmental influences to more positive ones, or changing your attachment towards the negative influences. This enables you to recognise further the Ego's unwanted involvement, to call it out, and to remove it from your thought-based influence.

If I couldn't break myself from the mental downward spiral, I would remove myself from the situation and do something completely different. The most effective way of doing this would be to pick up my garden shears and go out into the garden and trim something. This changed my state (doing something that I know I enjoy) and broke a cycle, giving me time to think more positively and create space to Reflect on what it is I am experiencing and what I want to experience in return.

The challenge of this technique is its simplicity. When we are really worked up or angry about something we tend to think that these simple techniques will have no value in very difficult situations. I can assure you that this technique is effective even in

FREE FROM FEAR

a more intense situation. In fact, the more difficult the situation, the more important it is to use these simple techniques, and they will be even more effective and more integral towards a happier, fear free life.

I would like to point out that if you learn to focus on the Present - the Now - any situation that requiring your intervention will simply cease to exist. Your state of Presence, coupled with your offering of love to all, can only produce one situation: a situation of Love. You get what you put out. The universe will provide that which you exude. What you put out, you get back - the basic principle of Karma.

The mastery of this approach, and your dedication to recognising the Ego within you and resolving its fear-based control over you, will ultimately rid you of any circumstances you may attract as being negative and replace them with positive, Love-based situations that will eventually lead to a level of abundance you truly deserve.

This goes for all people in all walks of life. The mastery of the Ego is the key to all abundance - be it happiness, fulfillment, successful relationships, or even material wealth. Fear is limiting. Love is forever expanding.

Fear is destructive. Love is creative. Fear is nothing but a mind-created illusion of control and oppression. Love is... Love.

Recognise

- Recognise what Fear-based constructs are arising within you.
- Place yourself in the other person's shoes to better understand their point of view.
- Recognise what Fear-based constructs are arising in them.

Reflect

- What is behind the Fear-based constructs arising in you and in the other person?
- Identify what Love-based response is most appropriate.
- Prepare yourself and your state of mind for implementing the Love-based response.

Resolve

- Implement your Love-based response.
- Analyse what mechanisms, rules or boundaries can be established to ensure a repeat of the situation doesn't occur again.

AndrewHackett.com.au

Cut this page out and put it on your fridge, cork board or on your workplace desk to provide a quick reference and reminder when you may need it the most.

Chapter Nine

Living in the Practical World

Being present is possibly one of the most difficult things a person can do - until they do; then it is easy. In being present, you either are or you are not. The question is: what is presence?

Presence is difficult to label, explain or understand. It's like explaining a state of being; you either are, or you are not. When you are, you don't really know if you are. In fact, in being present, you cannot know you are present, because in knowing you are present, you must not be, to have the thought about whether you are or not.

I use an analogy of "Being Spiritual." So many people today talk about being spiritual. They sometimes use their state of spirituality to pass judgement on others - or even to pass judgement on themselves. They take courses, workshops and weekend retreats in search of what it is to be spiritual. Always on the hunt, always looking for spirituality like it is a destination. It isn't.

Spirituality is not something for you to achieve. You cannot search for it because it isn't external to you. You either are being spiritual or you are not. It is almost the same as when people call Buddhism a religion. It isn't; it is more of a choice of being, a state of mind. Happiness is the same. There isn't a journey to be taken, or a path towards happiness. It is within you already. You just need to be still enough to listen to it.

Presence is no different. You either are being present or you are not. You cannot be both, but you can move from one to the other (sometimes hundreds of times a day). You can be present for seconds, sometimes minutes, rarely hours. Presence is broken up by states of unconscious mind chatter. It's "the Monkey mind."

I believe that presence is possibly best described as "a thoughtless state," or "a stillness within," which is often referred to as the Now.

Being truly present is about being in a state of consciousness that lives in the pinpoint of the immediately present time of right now. This very second. It is also eternal, it lasts forever and never

CHAPTER NINE

lives in the past or the future.

Like an endlessly rolling ball, the present point is as it touches the ground. It rolls down the road like a person lives through time. The present state is forever in the now, the point of which it touches the ground - never in front of it, never behind it, only at that point, forever, eternally rolling.

In the now, the past is nothing but a memory in your mind; the future is a projection of the memory into the possible. It is the point where you are connected to all that is. It is where magic happens.

Presence is perhaps best understood by witnessing examples of presence around us. Mother Nature is full of presence. Every moment, every minute, in every way. Trees are very present. They are only a tree - that is all they do and all they want to be. They live in the very moment of Now.

The duck on the pond is present. It only understands the present moment. Paddling away, bathing, drinking, foraging and eating. The duck forever lives in the present moment. I also find cows to be very present beings. Forever chewing on the grass, each second spent without fear of the past or the future. Beautifully calm creatures, doing what they do and nothing else. An animal's presence is seen in them being exactly who they are, whether it is the duck, the cow or the cat.

FREE FROM FEAR

Many spiritual teachers over the years have described animals as an eternal example of presence in everyday life. I believe this is true up to the point where human intervention impacts the animal's ability to be present. Having lived on a farm, I have seen this in all animals: the ducks, the cows and the sheep, and especially the varied birdlife. All present, living in the very point of time called the Now, until humans arrive. As incredibly intuitive creatures, they feed off our presence or lack thereof and read our present state, reacting accordingly.

I know from my own personal experience that living in the real world isn't easy. So much so that some people say, "If hell actually exists then this has got to be it!" I believe they were in fact closer to the mark than they realise.

Living in the practical world isn't easy – let me make that clear. In fact, it isn't easy for anyone; but it is not meant to be. Life in Heaven (or the spiritual realm) is easy, as it is only made up of pure divine Love. Everything you experience in that realm is constructed of Love. In the spiritual realm, we can *understand* life but not fully *experience* life and all it has to offer, because in Heaven the contrasts are not extreme enough for us to actually experience them; they only exist as concepts to enable us to understand them.

But here on earth, the physical world creates limitations. Fear

CHAPTER NINE

and the Ego reign in most lives, and that is why we chose to reincarnate here, on this Earth. What we fail to fully understand is that we can experience everything the physical world has to offer, including the pain and the fear, but we don't have to *suffer* from it; we don't have to let it consume us and run our lives. There is a way to stop the suffering, to stop the pain - and it is through the way we *think*.

We still need to chop the wood and carry the water. In fact, that is why we have chosen to be here. Being present means being practical, and it is essential to our overall experience.

What I mean here is that in the spiritual realm we can have what we want, whenever we want, and we can experience whatever our heart desires, with one simple exception: physicality. You cannot experience physicality in the spiritual dimension, and that is the primary reason why we choose to incarnate into a physical body. What it provides us is so amazing, so challenging and so incredible that we will want to do it over and over again - so much so, that you have already done so many times over.

In the physical space, both the experience of good and bad things is what our choice to incarnate is all about. We come to this planet to experience all that life has to offer, and through this process we learn to value all experiences equally, whether they are good or bad.

Floating off into the clouds, asking the universe to provide everything for you, and then sitting back on your bottom to do nothing about it is not going to work now, is it? We chose this existence; we also need to play by the basic rules of the physical world.

Everything pertaining to how we create our physical life is about **Thought, Statement and Action.** Many of us forget that the action bit is critical, because taking action is about living within the physical world. Yes, you have bills to pay. Yes, you have meals to prepare. You have children to raise, and you have to drive to work to earn the money to do all of that. That is the existence you have chosen to experience. It is a part of what we are here for: to chop the wood and carry the water.

We need to understand the role of practicality in our lives. Jumping off a cliff and using faith to stop you from hitting the bottom will only get you so far (usually, it takes you as far as to the bottom). Practicality is the key - and this is where a lot of people get lost. They lose their way and fail to realise their true, earthly potential.

It took me many years to understand the role of the practical side in my life, and when I did, I was thankful for this level of practicality. My practical nature is what has gotten me this far (albeit unconsciously). Practicality, coupled with a strong Faith, is

CHAPTER NINE

a force to be reckoned with. Then, if we add to that a conscious, creative desire to manifest, we have it: Pure Genius. Thoughts become real - even more so once we understand how and why.

The process of manifesting things in our life is simple and easy. In fact, we have all been doing it our entire lives - we have just not been aware of it. This is where the catch comes and why our thoughts are so important. A lot of us are manifesting unconsciously, and in doing so, our negative thoughts are manifesting things in our lives we don't want.

Let me explain the process of manifestation before we get into why it is so important to be consciously aware of our thoughts and how we use them to manifest either good or bad things in our life.

The process of manifestation is simple. It is traditionally a three-stage process of *Thought*, *Statement* and *Action*. I believe a fourth step of *Surrender* to the outcome is also integral to success, but I will cover that later in the book.

You see, your true *Thought* comes from the creative side of your soul. That is where all the great ideas come from. It is your inspiration, your God-given energy to create the life you want for yourself. We have to create the idea first.

The *Statement* is based on Faith: faith that it will be realised, faith that it is the right decision, and faith that you can manifest it into reality. The Statement is how you express your intention, and intention is the key to the success of this step. It really doesn't matter who the statement is made to, or how, or why; what really matters is the intention behind the statement. If the intention is true then the statement carries more weight. Faith is an important part of that, as it helps us enforce our intention. Although everything hinges on this Faith, the next step is where it really takes form.

The *Action* is 100% practicality. It is the hard work, the hard slog. It is the practical side of you that is necessary to get all things to manifest in the physical world. Everyone is capable, and everything is possible. You are as limitless as you believe yourself to be. But without the action, nothing is possible.

It was truly with this realisation that I started to see the power within me and why I have always felt like I was meant for better things - because I had just discovered the secret to life. Let me break it down a little further for you. Sit back and breathe and imagine this possibility...

You chose to come to this planet, to live this life for the experience, to experience yourself through your physical self-realisation. The whole point of coming to this planet is to experience the practical, physical-world aspects that are unique to this planet. The whole point is to experience the good *and* the bad. They are both as wonderful as each other.

CHAPTER NINE

If you have come here to experience all this, then surely you should embrace everything that also comes with it, the good and the bad, because are they not exactly what has brought you to this point? Keep in mind: you have possibly reincarnated many, many times – each time choosing a variation on the theme, to enable you to evolve spiritually through your everyday, practical, physical world experiences.

Some believe that when we choose to reincarnate, we choose which parents we wish to be born through, which determines our physical composition of the body we choose to occupy in this next life. Part of this belief is that we also choose a broad path of our life that we seek to achieve - a path that will enable us to grow in the areas we wish to evolve and to progress spiritually. This path isn't fixed, but preferred; and sometimes we enter into soul-based contracts with the key people in our lives that help shape our life as we currently know it.

I believe that we do, in fact, choose and map out a preferred path that is designed by us (our higher spiritual self) to enable us to grow and develop in a spiritually evolutionary sense to be the best we can possibly be. I believe that our intuition and the universe provides synchronistic events throughout our life to guide, and ultimately, to enable us to find and stay on our chosen path. I need to remember that I have chosen to experience and grow as an individual within the physical world I have chosen, so I must still "chop the wood and carry the water," so to speak. I can choose to live my life however I please, and I can choose to follow my path or not; but like any choice, there are consequences. I must understand that any failure to work within this practicality will create consequences that may not work well for my chosen path or direction.

Over the years I have seen a lot of spiritual people throw the towel in on their lives as a result of their awakening, disappearing to find themselves, to learn and to grow. They throw in their jobs, sell their house, and run off in search of happiness. While all that is very good and well, the problem is they often find themselves complaining about not having what they want - not having the material comforts that they fought so hard to let go of. They are no longer able to achieve what they desire. They believe they need to unchain themselves of the physical things in their lives, or that the material things are evil and not necessary. I would like to point out that it is not the physical things that are wrong, as there is nothing wrong with having things - just as long as one doesn't assign their self-worth or their internal value to such things. They are just things.

There is nothing wrong with having jobs, working in offices and doing what you are doing, as it is all part of the physical world

CHAPTER NINE

we choose to live in. Where so many people are falling short is they assign their own self-worth to such things, and when they realise that the things, the jobs, the status is not what makes them happy, they feel they need to throw it all away and start again. In fact, they only partially correct. They need to start again with the way they are *thinking* about themselves, the way they are assigning their worth to outwardly focused things.

The Porsche in the garage is not what makes them happy, but it is a lot of fun to drive. The senior management job isn't who they are, but it does earn enough income to deliver a certain physical-world comfort to their lives. What they hope for is happiness, peace and joy, and none of those feelings can come from things. None can be realised outwardly; they can only be realised inwardly.

This is where being practical is important - realising it is not only the world you live in, it is the experience you chose to experience. To disconnect from the reality of the physical world would only invite consequences that you may not be trying to manifest. The disconnection disrupts the energy flow that is the life experience as a whole. Now, if you want to throw everything away and experience life in a simple, reflective way without things and money, then great - do it. But understand that if you don't change your way of thinking then it will all be without the benefit you are seeking.

The key idea that needs to be shared with the world is that awakening is not just for the hippies, for the nature lovers and the wealthy people that don't have to worry about things like money. The awakening is remembering that we are all here to achieve what we desire to experience in life. Waking up and remembering why you are here and creating who you want to be can be done in the physical world: with bills and children, with mortgages and demanding family pressures. It can be done with all these things present in your life; in fact, it has to, for you to have realised the experience you set out to understand in the first place. Being present is the key.

I believe the meaning of life is that we are here to create life, *and* to experience it as we have created it. However we choose to is our choice. If we don't like it, if it doesn't make us happy, we can choose to change it - any aspect of it, or all of it. Some of us are choosing (consciously or unconsciously) to live life the way we are. Others choose a different experience. At any point in time, we can change it. Any point. The choice is always ours. Being present is the key, because without presence, we cannot fully understand what is truly working for us.

The awakening to the fact that we have choice is here - but too many people brush it off as too difficult, or as an unnecessary

CHAPTER NINE

interference. It appears to be in conflict with their lives, with what's important to them and what they have been *told* is actually important in their lives. I would like to point out that not only does it not need to be in conflict at all, it is actually very complimentary.

For instance, your day job (the most common conflicting aspect to a person's personal awakening experience) can provide immense benefits. It can provide the money you need to achieve what you set out to achieve, to build and create, to give and to honour, to serve and to love. Many people have chosen a job that enables them to give on a daily basis, like nurses, doctors, counsellors, community workers. Even the fixers (tradespeople), and the providers (retail and hospitality) provide valuable input towards the world - it just seems that not all people are aware that their job can provide something to humanity; or if they are aware, they are not thinking about it properly.

Ultimately, if your work does not serve you and your need to fulfil your spiritual desire, change it. Work somewhere else, do something else. Because once you are fulfilling your soul's physical-world agenda, then abundance will flow as you need. The trick is in staying present.

This also stands as sound advice in your relationships. If your relationship is not serving your truth, if it is not helping you move towards your chosen path, then you need to reconsider its value in your life. Sometimes cutting ties with an unhealthy relationship (even if it takes you back a few physical world steps) will move you forward spiritually if it is true to your chosen path. Time and time again I have heard people say that stepping out of an unhealthy relationship was the trigger that snapped them into waking up and realising their dreams. Often, through hitting rock bottom, we realise what is actually important to us, and it also gives us an obvious starting point from which to make change.

I know through my experience that my old day job felt like a lot of paper pushing without providing any benefit to humanity. However, by changing the way I thought about it, I started to realise that it gave me time to think, money to pay for the farm and to build my dream. It gave me the lifestyle I need to achieve all that I have. It paid me well for very little output, providing me with other benefits to enable me to grow and build while still meeting the practical-world needs of my life experience.

Furthermore, my old job (the one not providing much value to humanity) just needed to be rethought. I soon realised that I could use over 20 years of experience to teach people how to achieve what they want in their life, thereby providing a service to humanity while realising a lifelong dream. This is but a step along the future path, which is why I came to this planet in the first place.

Through all this I needed to realise: I have bills to pay, so I

CHAPTER NINE

need to chop the wood and carry the water, because that is what living on this planet is all about. That shouldn't stop anything - it shouldn't stop me from doing what my heart truly calls out for, because if it does then I am not thinking about it right.

The practical world you live in is an important aspect of your current physical manifestation. As I stated in the previous chapter, finding and maintaining our state of Presence is important to managing the mind and it's egoic diatribe. Accordingly, the first tool you need to learn about ties in with your state of presence. The state of presence is important to understand and utilise as it helps you see everything for what it is. When in a present state, normal physical egoic tools lose their value in the day-to-day, which means their place in your associated value system diminish. For instance, while in your state of presence, the Ferrari in the garage becomes just a car, not a status symbol. The senior management job is just a job, not a symbol of power. The stock portfolio just a retirement tool, not a sign of how successful or important you are. Nothings has changed in the physical sense, only in your way of associating to them - and that is the point.

For all things to become possible, first of all your point of view must change. Practicing your presence will ultimately facilitate this, but so will understanding the reality of where you are and why you are here - and I don't mean that quite the way you may think.

FREE FROM FEAR

What I mean is: you have chosen this physical existence because it enables you to learn and experience many things you cannot experience in the spiritual world. So, first of all you need to understand and accept that everything that is happening to you is because you chose it to be so. You made a conscious decision to take on board this physical body, to experience this physical dimension, to grow as a spiritual being, in more ways than your physical mind can possibly understand.

In understanding that "it is as you have chosen it to be" the obvious realisation is to accept everything that comes across your path as part of that choice. Then you need to stop and breathe to better understand why this particular event, moment or problem is happening to you - what you want to make of it, what you want to create from it, or what you want to learn, understand and grow from it. Understanding this concept and surrendering to it is key to the fear in your life falling away.

Secondly, everything that you experience within the physical context is just a manifestation of your desires and nothing more. Everything you experience, and how you experience it, is completely your doing, your manifestation, and completely within your control. So everything - right down to the bad day you are having - is part of your physical-world process of growth that your eternal soul has chosen to experience.

CHAPTER NINE

The exciting part of this understanding is that not only can everything have a purpose, but that it doesn't need to have a negative purpose. In fact, you will start to realise that everything has a divine purpose; and if that is the case, then everything that happens is perfect, in the way everything in the universe is perfect. Even the really bad days.

What I mean by this is: not only does everything that comes into your existence have a positive possibility towards your present state, but since everything in your physical context is a manifestation of your state of mind, you are in complete control of everything that happens to you.

You can manifest anything, at anytime, for any purpose. The purpose doesn't need to be divine, good or righteous. People everywhere, every day, manifest things that they perceive to be bad for them (albeit unconsciously) or bad for others - or at least, not contributing to the greater good. We say *perceive* for a very good reason: because it is all in the perception; because the universe doesn't judge. It doesn't need to be. It knows everything is perfect in every sense of the word.

Highly-evolved beings all understand that everything happens for a reason. What we humans need to understand is: "What is it that we are to learn from this experience that we are currently experiencing?" Highly-evolved beings always find positive value in every experience, irrespective of how terrible it could be perceived as by someone else. There is always something positive to be found in every experience.

So let's talk again about our presence. The purpose of being present is to calm the mind-based, egoic and fear-driven chatter in our heads: to enable an opportunity for calm peacefulness to rise within us, so we can listen to our intuition more easily. As time passes, your ability to connect to your intuition (even in noisy, highly emotionally-charged situations) will be easy, if not second nature; and ultimately this enables us to better understand everything that crosses your paths. I believe if we can breakdown to the rawest basic construct of what everything is, it enables us to understand things for what they are (hopefully without projecting fear upon it) and why they are presenting in our lives.

They say breaking or creating a habit takes three weeks. I understand that to turn a habit (positive or otherwise) into an unconscious behavioural pattern it takes consistent regular application over a period of twelve weeks. If you practice anything consistently for three weeks you will create a habit. For twelve weeks, the practicing will become a subconscious behavioural pattern. Now, if you want to make significant positive changes in your life, break your old habits and set new, positive ones. Furthermore, turn those new positive habits into solid,

CHAPTER NINE

subconscious behavioural traits that serve you and the life you wish to live. The same can be said in your practicing being present. Practicing your presence will enable the process to become second nature in time, and will facilitate achieving your state of presence by removing the distracting, fear-based interferences you experience in your daily physical world.

The process of being present is important because it enables us to disconnect from the unhealthy Ego and stay connected to all that is. I believe that understanding what is happening around us is a good first step. Meditation is a good way to become present, and I highly recommend that we all find at least twenty minutes every day to practice proper meditation because its effects can be very beneficial to the mind and the body. However, you can be present at anytime, anywhere and in any situation. Some people sit quietly and focus on a particular object or point in the room. Some pick a positive phrase or chant and repeat it over and over again to calm the mind.

Practical Presence is a mindfulness meditation often practiced by Buddhist monks when they focus on the activity they are doing so completely that they don't allow any other thoughts to enter their present state. This might mean they focus on each step they take when they walk, enjoying it for everything that it delivers to them in this physical world. You can do it when you sweep the paths outside, when you bring in your firewood in winter, or even when you wash the dishes like I do. There are many books on this subject from Thich Nhat Han or Eckhart Tolle that I can recommend. They are worth exploring.

Practical Presence enables the individual to disassociate themselves from their own internal value with things or events that happen that don't require association. It is recommended as a meditation at first; then, try to do it whenever you have a quiet moment. Understand everything that is around you, and every event as, and when, it happens. Remember: don't allow fear-based egoic stories and chatter to enter your mind.

Practice your Practical Presence every day and from it will come an understanding of things and events around you, bringing a level of clarity that you will learn to love. Learn to understand that despite what is going on around you, you are O.K. - you are safe, you have already survived many of these events to date, and you were doing so *unconsciously*. Imagine what you can achieve with a *conscious* approach to understanding the things and events that crop up in your daily life!

Practical Presence is quite a powerful tool to enable fear to fall away in your life. It will eventually bring peace and joy to your heart like you have never experienced before. When you are truly present you begin to understand that all is well in your life; that

CHAPTER NINE

you are safe, and always have been; that everything that happened to you was to create the fabulous person you are now, and to enable you to be the person required to achieve whatever it is you want to achieve.

Fears usually arrives in our lives by events, or the mind's memory of past events that the Ego wants to self-perpetuate. Understanding them as they appear is the key to mastering presence and disconnecting the Ego from its influence over you within each moment. Being present in a controlled environment is easy. For example: at work, or in a yoga class in a quiet space, like a library. However, being present in the company of your family and friends can be very difficult because they can easily trigger your egoic responses and fear-driven thought processes. This occurs more often in your home, or amongst friends or family. This often happens in family disputes, arguments with friends, or when someone challenges your authority. For parents, your kids are your most important testing ground. Maintaining presence while your kids are testing your nerves, or while you are dealing with moody teenagers, can be some our biggest challenges. It certainly has been for me!

Using a technique such as Practical Presence is important because when fear is at play in an outwardly aggressive way, the emotional triggers within your mind and the physical triggers within your body are often heightened; therefore, you have other elements to break down and understand. This often takes immense self-understanding and incredible self-control. This ties into the earlier-mentioned technique of Recognise, Reflect and Resolve. The purpose of the technique is to give an alternative thought process for the mind to focus on. It also helps you to understand what is going on and allows an almost meditative state of mind to take over, enabling you to more easily keep calm and relaxed in confrontational situations.

So, working through the process of the Practical Presence technique, first we need to remind ourselves to breathe deeply; to enable a pause in our egoic association to the difficult events that may be unfolding; and allow a few seconds to reflect on what is going on. Bear in mind, this is very difficult for any physical being to do. Please don't judge yourself if it's not coming together easily, because it isn't easy.

Breathe, breathe again, and try to stop and notice what is going on. Breathe again, and please don't stop those big deep breaths! Focus on your breathing if that helps - I know it does for me! When you have settled your mind, focus on what is happening within you. What emotions are you feeling right now? What thoughts are their words or actions triggering within you? Label them, without judgement - just factual understandings of what

CHAPTER NINE

those thoughts or emotions are, and be honest with yourself. Is it anger, frustration, guilt, shame? Are you afraid you are going to lose something, or is it just simply that egoic beast rising within you that makes you not want to give ground, not understand their point of view, or not let go of something you have fought hard for?

Second, try and notice what is happening with *them*. What thoughts and feelings are they expressing? What triggers are they experiencing? Are they very similar? Is it fear- driven or simply their ego? Is it possibly both?

The purpose of this is to *Recognise* what fear constructs are at play, not only in yourself but also in the others present. The clarity from knowing what is happening around you will help immensely. If you cannot understand their side of things, don't worry - just focus on yourself and understand that. Recognition of your own experiential constructs is important. Use the breath to not only afford you time to understand, but then use it to *Reflect* on those constructs you are experiencing. Eliminate which ones are not serving you and zero in on which ones will enable you to return to a present state. Usually those will be constructs of Love.

Who is this person to you? Family, or friend? There must be things you love about this person, things that show you that this matter is worth resolving. Look for ways that you can change their emotional state, like a smile, a reassuring comment or even a touch or a big hug. Tell them something positive, something reassuring. Break the negative Fear cycle and move towards a positive Love cycle.

This isn't about giving in, giving ground, or giving up on your point of view. It is about utilizing better techniques to enable your words to be heard, not defended against. It is about showing, through a change in presence, that there is a better way - a calmer, loving way. Recognising what is happening within you can enable you to recognise what is happening in another. Through this process you can then *Reflect* on what approach may work to diffuse the situation, to change the emotional state of the other person. Already at this point you are thinking more clearly and less reactively. You are able to change what is happening for the better. Through a calming, more loving approach, you will also find yourself less positional, less confrontational, and less needing of your Ego to be stroked and applauded. This in turn will also change the energy of the other person, and they will slowly realise the same factors within themselves, even if only unconsciously. Now, think of how you can *Resolve* the situation.

Don't let the Ego trick you into thinking that the other person should be doing something here, or even meeting you halfway. The Ego will also try to get you to assume that the other person is capable (or should be capable) of understanding how to turn it

CHAPTER NINE

around. But it is up to you. It is your experience and your life. So do something positive about this negative fear-based presence you find yourself in.

Using your opportunity of reflection to find a way to change their state, and work towards a path to *Resolve*, right here, in the Now, is where it all matters. Don't be dissuaded if the other party is still too worked up to come to the table with your proposed solution to reconcile the situation. Try changing the state again, and keep trying. Be gentle, soft and loving. In the presence of light, darkness cannot exist; so it shouldn't take too long. It will always work eventually.

I am not saying they will see your viewpoint, or accept that you are right and they are wrong. That is not what this is about. It is about understanding what is happening to you, to enable you to resolve within yourself what isn't working for you. To bring back your state of presence, and to use that presence to resolve the Fear-based constructs. To remove egoic tendencies, and revert to constructs of Love as a way of living your life, as a way of offering yourself to others. To enable them to let go of their Fear-based constructs and resolve within them what is necessary. At the very least, you won't be scared, or fearful of what is happening.

The first few times you have to practice this it will all feel very surreal. I know, as I have practiced it on family quite a bit. They never knew what I was doing, but they did appreciate the results in the end.

I have also had a few occasions to practice this when confronted with highly emotionally-charged individuals that were beyond angry, fuming in their egoic Fear- based ways. Although each event was unrelated, each played out in the same way, rather surprisingly. Each event started with a lot of very aggressive behaviour, which escalated very fast indeed. I was initially surprised at how fast things got very out of control. On each occasion that I faced the possibility of being assaulted or physically harmed, I focused on remaining present as my number one priority. As they yelled and screamed their point of view (a point of view that had been building up for some twelve months or more) I just maintained a non-confrontational posture. I focused on my breathing, avoided eye contact and gently acknowledged each point they made. I made a conscious point to not react, but only to offer thoughts of love and peace in their direction.

As time passed they calmed down - in fact, they seemed to forget what triggered it all in the first place. Then they forgot the position that they were arguing so aggressively, and started to wonder what all the fuss was about. Their obvious rage was only changed with a Love-based construct. I continued to offer them that in the days following. I chose not to ever make my point

CHAPTER NINE

because it was irrelevant anyway. I accepted my role in the situation, offered them (via thoughts in my mind) love in recognition of their suffering. When they later returned to apologise for their behaviour, I told them to think nothing of it. I explained to them I have also been angry about things in the past, I have also lashed out at others, and I wasn't in any position to pass judgement on them about anything.

An interesting note to make on this matter is that you don't always have to be with the other party to offer them thoughts of love and peace. The souls are not on the physical plane and are in fact omnipresent, meaning, in all places at all times in all possible ways. An ancient Hawaiian practice of reconciliation and forgiveness (called Ho'oponopono) is a very effective way to offer love and peace into a situation that cannot be resolved through direct physical communication. It is a practice that offers and seeks forgiveness at a soul-based level, that communicates from one soul to the other whether the other party is aware of it or not.

The simple prayer is: "I love you, I'm sorry, please forgive me, thank you."

I have personally used this on many occasions, sitting quietly, meditating on the person involved, repeating this prayer over and over. It is extraordinarily powerful.

Please keep in mind that you can use this phrase or another;

the real power in in the offering of love and forgiveness to the other, which is communicated and received at a soul-based level between the parties. You can use whatever words you feel are most relevant to the situation, but ensure that the words you use are strictly constructs of Love and not Fear.

This technique is often through the understanding that by "being" is through example, not evangelism. Evangelism is an act of the ego, not Love. It is through "being," not instructing; it is showing through "being" that is the key. *Being* is through pure action, not through statements of what should be, or what you are going to do. What I mean by this is: you will always be able to show more through "being" a construct of Love. Not through explaining. The action, not the words. You will always resolve more through "being" a construct of love. Again, because it happens in the omnipresent sense, at a soul-based cellular level. Because when you are being from a presence of love then others around you will start to do so, too (either consciously or unconsciously). They will feel it, just as they feel attacked when you are angry and yelling and screaming at them. You know how powerful an energy it is when someone is yelling and screaming and carrying on. Love is more powerful than Fear, as is being Love when Fear is at it loudest.

So don't talk about it, don't speak it, be it. *Be it.* That is what

CHAPTER NINE

being is about.

It is through this being in the presence of love that you can start to understand what Love Presence is all about. There is no pulpit, there is no soapbox, because that is what the Ego wants. There is no thanks, there is no acknowledgement, because that is what the Ego desires, too.

Focus your presence on the practicality of the physical life you have chosen to experience. Focus your energy on positive thoughts, but don't lose sight of what is required of you in your real-world existence, the physical existence. Don't forget to chop the wood and carry the water. This is the key to living in the present state. Being present will open up the world at your feet, but being practical while being present will keep the bills in check, the house cleaned and the children fed while the world is opening up at your feet.

True Presence is found in a state of pure unconditional love, and it is beautiful, divine and very achievable. It is literally one simple choice away. This process is not just about teaching you. It is not just about showing you how it is done. It is about explaining that just through being practical while in your state of Love Presence, you are, in fact, being Love.

Presence is the key to everything. But remember that being present in the silent comfort of a controlled environment is easy.

FREE FROM FEAR

The master strives for Love Presence in the most difficult of situations, the most confrontational, the most fear-influenced events. Not because they will have finally mastered it, but because it will shine the brightest of lights in the darkest of halls.

We should reach out to those whose frequency is different to ours. We should reach out to those whose minds are filled with fear-based chatter to listen, and love, and be present in their company. Don't feed their pain bodies. Don't feed their drama-based stories. Just love and offer compassion. Be present, and love.

The master desires the Love Presence because the master knows that the mere presence of Love dispels any possibility of Fear. To do this in the physical world is the ultimate mastery: on Earth as it is in Heaven. Each aspect assists the other, and together it is the most powerful force in the universe. Love Presence can manifest anything at anytime.

This state of being is the way of the Budda. It is the way of the Christ Consciousness, it is Krishna, Jesus, Mohammad and you. It is in all of those beings, and it is within you.

ANDREW HACKETT

Love Presence

Stop.

Breath.

What am I experiencing now?

As I chose this moment what is happening within me now?

Breath.

Are any Fear-based constructs at play now?

Is my Ego at play?

What Love-based constructs can I choose to experience instead?

Can I enjoy what is happening now?

I am responsible for the experience I am having.

I appreciate what I can learn from this situation.

I am grateful for the life I have chosen.

AndrewHackett.com.au

Cut this page out and put it on your fridge, cork board or on your workplace desk to provide a quick reference and reminder when you may need it the most.

Chapter Ten

Manifestation for the Busy Person

Manifesting what you want in your life is not possible. That is a simple truth. It will only leave you with the experience of wanting, because that is what you are feeling... *wanting*. This is based on the notion that whatever we put out, we get back. It ties in with the "do unto others" notion that how we treat others is how we are treated by others. The basic breakdown of this is that every thought we have is sent out to the universe, noted, and returned via the experiences and interactions we have with the world around us.

It is a relatively simple notion, but often forgotten in day-to-day application. Every thought you have creates the experience you call life. Most people are too focused on complaining about others, the traffic, or their life situation. They don't have enough, or others have more. They can't find love, or people are always trying to crack onto them. They think people are ugly, insensitive, or doing something wrong. They hate themselves, are guilty of something, or feel shame about something else. It's no wonder so many of us are unhappy. The simple fact remains: it doesn't have to be that way. There is only one person who is completely responsible for your experience of life - *You*. And it has everything to do with the way you are thinking.

To understand this, we must accept the premise that we create everything through the very thoughts we have. What we think, in its literal sense, creates what we experience. We can also choose not to accept it, but the rule still stands: we will still attract what we think about. Our experience is shaped by how we feel about what we think about. Accept it or not, it still happens and will forever continue to happen. If fact, it has happened your entire life. You were just unconscious of it.

My thought process is based around a simple idea. If I am manifesting my life *unconsciously*, imagine what can be achieved if I am doing it *consciously*. Imagine the possibilities. It is true. I have proven it, and it is repeatable in others. I'm not the first to prove it. It has been stated over and over for centuries, but I am

CHAPTER TEN

here to tell you now, again. What you think, and how you feel about it, *creates*. Quite literally.

Our thoughts are the creative mechanism that tells the universe what we wish to experience. So, when we are having thoughts of sadness, inadequacy, lack or hatred, we tell the universe through our thoughts that this is what we want to experience. Then we become sad, people dislike us, inadequacy appears and the experience of lack results. How we treat others signals the universe that this is how we want to be treated, so not surprisingly that is how people treat us. Every thought, creates.

So on that premise, accepting that in the overall space/time continuum you already have everything you need at any given time (and being grateful for that fact) is actually the key to manifesting everything. What you put out you get back. If you want, you are left with the experience of wanting. If you "have" then you are left with the experience of having, and it is left to the physical world's laws of space, time and matter to deliver it into your physical existence. That is where you come in.

This theory is discussed by many ancient and modern spiritual teachers throughout the world. It is true and really worth exploring here. Understanding the basics of the laws of attraction will not only help you manifest success and wealth in your life, but it will also help you manifest happiness, peace and unconditional love in your life. Additionally, it is part of the process of removing Fear - and the influence Fear has over you - from your life.

Before we get into the detail, let's first understand the basics of manifesting. There are four key steps to manifesting anything in your life: **Thought**, **Statement**, **Action** and **Surrender**.

Your **Thoughts** comes from the creative side of your soul; that is where all the great ideas come from. It is your inspiration, your God-given energy to create the life you want for yourself. The Thought is the idea in its initial creative concept, built on and developed as a deliverable idea. Without the idea, nothing can happen.

The **Statement** is your commitment to the universe that sets your intention and is your command to the universe to create it. It is often based on faith - faith that it will be realised, faith that it is the right decision, and faith that you can manifest it into reality. In fact, it is faith that it has already been decided, and that all you need to do is create the physical-world actions to enable it to appear. Although everything hinges on this Faith and the intention behind it, the next step is where it really takes form, because it is in the physical world where it all manifests.

The **Action** is 100% practicality; it is the hard work, the hard slog. It *is* the intention and statement manifested. It is the practical side of you that is necessary to get all things to manifest in the

CHAPTER TEN

physical world. Everyone is capable, and everything is possible. It is as limitless as you believe yourself to be. But without the action, nothing is possible. This needs to be understood with one simple rule in the physical world: you need to respect the physical-world constructs that allow everything to come into play. Action is the one thing that separates successful people from the rest of us.

Then you need to **Surrender** your attachment to the outcomes of the statement you have made to the universe, and engage your Faith that it is on its way. This Faith is as important as the steps you take towards achieving it. Unshakeable belief that it will manifest, coupled with the action on every step needed to create it, will guarantee its success. Surrendering to the outcome of the universe is important, because the universe truly knows all - and by surrendering to the notion that it will arrive exactly when it is needed, you signal to the universe that you accept that it is already delivered, and that physical time is all you are waiting for. I refer to the faith applied at this point in time as Infinite Patience. With Infinite Patience applied, everything arrives exactly when it is supposed to.

Now all of this sounds wonderful, and easy, and in fact it is, but what does it all mean? Can I just say that I want a private jet, and it appears out of thin air? No. This is because your wanting will leave you with exactly that, wanting; and that is simply not

FREE FROM FEAR

how this works.

This process requires practice, like any aspect of personal development. Like a muscle, it needs training and development. I recommend you start out small and work your way up. This is primarily because it will build up your confidence and add to the belief structure that it is not only possible, but that you can do it.

Furthermore, additional minds speed things up. It's like when someone believes in something it can only happen at the pace of one person. But if three people believe, or ten, it happens faster with the collective thoughts and energy of many applied. With hundreds, amazing things can happen; with thousands, governments can be overthrown, and millions? Well, life as we know it can change for the betterment of all. This process is no different.

The reason for this is four-fold. First, the idea must be created. This usually happens at a point of origin, but it is possible that two or more people can have the same idea at the same time. Whether they connect with each other early enough is irrelevant and part of the universe's magic. Once the idea is developed and shared through the statement stage, others become aware of it. Their thoughts can manifest on it and give it energy. Working groups can be formed to help build on the intention.

This also breeds interest in others. Statements can involve

CHAPTER TEN

marketing the idea, advertising or using social networking to get the word out. This also adds more energy to it. When the action step comes into play, many people may be involved, leaders step up to lead, and massive action is taken on a great scale. With these sorts of numbers, there is no single point of attachment to the outcome to create a negative expectation around its delivery; the attachment to the outcome is shared or non- specific, so the surrendering is naturally, unconsciously accepted.

We have many examples of this throughout history - great ideas, manifested into the reality of thousands. We are seeing it today with the spiritual movement, awakening thousands around the world every day. The collective consciousness given to a single idea is one of the most powerful acts there is. It is available to us every day, and we must accept it as not only a possibility but as a factual part of our everyday existence. It is where miracles happen.

Look back on your life and look at anything you have achieved. You will notice that (unconsciously perhaps) you have followed this process all along. The problem is that this is the same process that creates all the negative things in our life. The universe doesn't judge, and you are the creator. It just delivers.

We need to be careful, because the manifestation of negative experiences can happen just the same way. If many people have a collective thought of negativity it can just as likely happen. Acts of terrorism are built on this premise. If they can create enough fear within the general population, that fear can take a hold, and this is how wars start.

At this point we need to understand the power of the ego, the need to transcend it, and more importantly, to collectively understand the power of offering Love to Fear-based constructs, not judgement. Dealing with the fear in your life is also through the same practice. Identify the fear, focus on the thought of no longer having that fear in your life, and focus on desiring a fear-free life. See how it makes you feel, being free from fear. The peaceful or joyful feeling it creates is the strong signal to the universe of what you truly desire, and the universe will respond in kind with like experiences.

Make the statement to yourself: that you no longer allow fear in your life. Pay close attention when the Ego battles for your attention, and offer the Ego your love. Tell the Ego you no longer require its influence in your daily life and that you have decided to be free from its fear-driven ways. Focus on positive thoughts about everything you do, stop complaining and start seeing the good that exists in all things, experiences and beings. When fear arises again (with the Ego or not) repeat the process.

We need to understand that manifestation is about the projection of the intuitive desire through the Now. The difference

CHAPTER TEN

in many is subtle; in some, the difference is vast. Again, maintaining your presence is important. Choosing a Love Presence is even more important.

But I am here to help you know that it doesn't take thousands or millions of minds to manifest things in your life. I know. I have done it, time and time again. At first unconsciously; but now I exercise it on a daily basis, to great effect. It only takes one person, and that person is you.

If you want to speed up the process of manifestation that the universe returns to you, there is a faster path to manifesting. This path involves following the process above, with the addition of a process that involves you enabling in another's life what you seek to achieve in your own. This is a physical-world mechanism of the "do unto others concept" that is built on the premise that what we put out, the universe sends back. If you seek to improve your financial situation, help someone else improve theirs. Give money away to a homeless person, or donate to a good cause. This not only sends a signal to the universe that you are generous and kind to another; it also says that you are already wealthy enough to have spare money enough to give to another. This sends a message to the universe that you are wealthy, causing wealth energy to flow more abundantly.

If you desire a promotion or a change in career, help another who desires the same thing to achieve it, and the universe will receive that amplified signal - and not just the signal of the desire itself (which is stronger with two hearts experiencing it) but also the amplified signals of love, caring, stewardship and altruism. They are all strong signals of Love constructs that compound the energy needed for manifesting. Compounding helps manifesting grow - for you, for them, and for those around you.

What we need to know from this example is that through causing another to feel something wonderful - like wealth, the happiness coming from someone caring for them, generosity or abundance - you clearly signal to the universe in the strongest possible context that that is what you want to experience in your life. The feelings you cause in another magnify the signal out to the universe because it comes from two hearts. This is also further magnified from the incredibly joyful feeling it produces in you, which amplifies the universe's response back towards you. Try this. I promise you, it works.

Now, keep in mind at all times that the process of manifestation is received literally from the universe, and granted literally. It stands to reason that it is also used, either consciously or unconsciously, to create negative experiences in one's life. Enabling another to manifest negative experiences magnifies the negative energy the universe returns, and the feeling it produces

CHAPTER TEN

also further magnifies. I believe this is what is referred to in some cultures as Karma. I can also confirm that this technique works to create pain and suffering in the world.

As with all things, practice makes perfect. Practice with love, as often as possible, whenever possible. Get your partner involved, and your family and friends. The more people involved, focusing on great deeds from Love-based constructs, the more the universe will respond, the quicker the universe will respond, and the faster the world will change for the better.

ANDREW HACKETT

Thought

Understand what I desire to manifest in my experience.
What does it look like?
How does the realisation of this make me feel?

Statement

I am grateful for (what you're trying to manifest) appearing in my life's experience.

Action

What actions are required for me to take to open the doors to the realisation of what I am manifesting?
TAKE ACTION NOW.

Surrender

I have faith that the universe will provide whatever is necessary for (what you're trying to manifest) to appear in my life's experience.

AndrewHackett.com.au

Cut this page out and put it on your fridge, cork board or on your workplace desk to provide a quick reference and reminder when you may need it the most.

Chapter Eleven

Some Takeaways for the Soul

If what we feel or experience is either based on Love or Fear, the intention we attach to that experience creates the outcome, which presents in the physical sense as either Pleasure or Pain. The experience of Pleasure or Pain is usually the result of certain rules we have constructed throughout our lifetime. It is purely a construct of the environment we were raised in. In other words, the rules are created by our interpretation of our upbringing. The problem is that as our lives change over the years these rules often no longer serve us. The trick is to get to know these rules and analyse them to determine which ones are serving you - and which are not.

Once we know what our rules are we can associate current,

everyday events to the emotional context within our feelings that are created by them. This allows us to break down what is happening, distance ourselves from an emotionally-negative response, and focus our energy on the way we want to react. Once we understand the emotional state we desire to experience we can implement that desire instead of an egoic emotional response born from fear.

Once we know our rules we are in a better position to locate, or associate, the rules others may have and give ourselves a better opportunity to understand them in any event of confrontation or disagreement. Through our understanding of the other person's personal driver, we can better understand what is happening in them and react appropriately. I have always said, "If I can understand the thought process they have gone through to reach a specific outcome, I can respect that. Even if I don't agree with it, I can respect it."

By putting yourself in their shoes you can better understand their thought process; but to be able to do that, we first need to gain control of our own emotional response. This process often enables a person to disconnect from the emotional, fear-based, egoic process that leads to the breakdown of the situation and gives them an opportunity to better understand the other person's point of view.

CHAPTER ELEVEN

If it can be done in a pure state of presence, this method can be taken to a whole new level. A spiritual connection can be established between you and the other person and you can literally look from their eyes, feel their feelings, and understand what is happening within them that is leading to the fear-based situation. This is done by viewing the situation from their point of view. This spiritual connection can best be described as an intentional connection between your higher self and their higher self, through the Love-constructed intention of wanting a better outcome for all parties involved. Although this can happen unconsciously, it is better for it to happen consciously, even if only by one side of the equation.

Please understand: this is very difficult to master, because the Ego is usually in full swing, and the Ego doesn't want a healthy resolution. The Ego wants control. The Ego wants conflict and disconnection, through which it can control with fear-based mechanisms. Therefore, it must self-perpetuate the madness to maintain its own existence. A level of self-control or self-understanding is required to stay present in this situation, and this can only be achieved through dedication, meditation and practice.

Maintaining a state of presence is important to enabling all of this to succeed. It is also the most difficult thing to do in a situation where you are well-practiced in losing control of any state of presence and succumbing to fear-based behaviours. This has been (what I can easily say) my greatest challenge - staying present, and keeping the Ego out of my mind, when I am challenged with situations that traditionally create stress, fear or confrontation. This is even more difficult when you are emotionally- bonded to the outcome being a certain way, or too invested in the outcome.

There are some tools you can adopt to help you stay present, and these are **Breathing**, **External Viewing** and **External Assignment**. I can promise you, if you understand, practice and implement these processes in your life, not only will you remove fear from your interactions, you will also make friends, be successful, and feel happy each and every day.

Breathing

Breathing may be an obvious one, because it can enable the person to reconnect back to their present state. It also enables the person to reconnect and opens up the channels for inspiration and guidance from their spirit guides, the universe, or God (depending on your belief systems). Breathing is a known technique that has physical benefits of slowing the adrenaline rush within the body, as well as calming the heart rate and effectively reducing the impact of the adrenaline-fueled fight or flight response that is inherent in all of us.

CHAPTER ELEVEN

The breathing process is taking three big breaths, breathing in through the nose (filling the lungs and diaphragm up completely), pausing at the top of the breath, and then breathing out until completely empty. After a short pause again, repeat the process. This can be done quietly if in the company of aggressive people, but it is important to practice this each and every time a confrontational situation arises. Like the practice of any discipline, the more practice given to this simple technique, the quicker it will become second nature and will happen automatically for you.

I like to do it whenever a frustration arises. In the car, when someone is driving slowly or you're stuck in traffic. When dealing with difficult customers at work. When frustrated at the kids who are being noisy and you want some quiet to think clearly. Repeating this practice whenever you can develops an unconscious habit that triggers whenever you feel stressed or anxious. This slowly reverses the feelings that trigger when you are in these situations. Breathing in opens up the body, the air clears the thoughts in the head, and the body takes in much needed oxygen, atoms and particles. Breathing out relaxes the body and expels fear-created toxins from the system. This practice is an easy one to master in moments when you are on your own, but essential to master prior to trying it with other confronting people present.

The process of acknowledging when you are feeling

frustrated, angry, anxious, or simply bothered is a good place to start this breathing process. This is because after the acknowledgement has been realised you start to focus on the process of settling the body away from the "fight or flight" process you have learned from a young age. This in turn creates enough of a break in the state of mind to enable you to start the process of Recognition, Reflection and Resolution. The breathing technique is an easy way to move through this process, and a good point to enable the process to start.

Once you have settled the adrenaline a little, and are a little calmer and clearer in the mind, you are in the state of being able to Recognise what is going on around you. You can start to look at the other person's point of view through their eyes (understanding their motivations, their Fear constructs, or their needs that drive the Fear-based constructs). At this point it is also important to understand what is happening within you and identify what Fear-based constructs you are experiencing, as well. Identifying these will enable you to call the Ego to account, offering it Love, while you remind it you are no longer interested in its poisonous ways, dispelling its relevance to this situation.

Once this Recognition process has been realised you now have more information at hand to better understand how to deal with the situation. That then enables you to work towards the

CHAPTER ELEVEN

process of Reflection. In other words, you can start to break down the information at hand to better understand the path towards a Love-focused resolution. Remember: Love is the disarming tool of all Fear-based constructs, and the focus on a Love-based approach is important. Don't try to add too much logic at this stage, as the Ego can interfere with the logical reasoning process. During the Reflection stage we need to start asking, "What would Love do here?" or, "How would Love approach this situation?" In asking the question we literally open up the channels to our intuitive based system of recognition, calling for help from the universe, if you will. But here comes the tricky bit, and here is where staying present is vital.

If you have managed to work through this process, you have hopefully managed to reach a point of being calm, clear-headed and present. If this is the case you should be able to hear your intuition talking or guiding you towards a response. That response, if followed, will lead you through the reconciliation process that best suits the situation. Why would that be the case, I hear you ask? Well, that's where this starts to get really cool.

Your spirit guides (or, your higher self) are only beings of light. Therefore, they can only produce guidance associated with light and love-based ideals. But they have a big advantage in this situation. They know the person you are dealing with is also a part of Love, just as you are; therefore, they are fundamentally of light and love also. They know this because they are in cahoots with the other person's spirit guides to ensure that the situation is resolved in a loving way, so that all parties can learn from the process of Love Reconciliation. They also know everything about the situation, as well as the resolution, and all events that stem from the outcomes, however it resolves. The catch is: you need to be present enough to be calm and clear-headed enough to listen to their guidance in the first place. It is a little bit like the chicken or the egg thing, but it is an important matter to understand correctly.

The number one, fundamental reason why you never see this happening in the real world is because we are taught to be reactive, irrational and Ego-driven beings. Many of our world leaders know how easy it is to control the masses through fear - a process that, along with control, also gives them relevance and superiority. If they were to govern people with an enlightened love-based societal model, there would be no need for governments, police, armies or the military industrial complex at all. In fact, the entire world could be overseen by a handful of highly-enlightened beings and peace would reign - as would happiness and joy.

Some people say that this would destroy freedom of choice or free will. On the contrary, that would never change; the society

CHAPTER ELEVEN

could still operate by exercising our right to free will, through choices associated to Love-based constructs. Through this approach, not only would world peace reign, but you would eliminate poverty, hunger and fear entirely for each and every human being on the planet. In fact, through this approach, the earth could provide enough abundance for tens of billions of more humans and everyone would have everything they ever needed.

The other reason why you rarely see this happen is because rarely is anyone calm and relaxed enough in a situation of conflict to be able to listen carefully and quietly to their intuitive thoughts - even more so for two people to do the same. However, the success of this method of resolving conflict (or at the very least, your attachment to the outcome of the conflict) is not dependant on both people participating in the process. It is only dependant on *you* staying present, calm and working through the process. When you do, the love and light you add to the situation will help towards calming the other person - maybe enough to move towards a resolution of the conflict or disagreement.

External Viewing

External Viewing is the process where you consciously pause in the middle of the process to visualise yourself leaving your body and rising above or beside the situation to better understand the mechanisms at play. The element of detaching yourself from your physical body also enables you to disconnect yourself from the physical-world, Fear-based constructs long enough to work through the process of Recognise, Reflect and Resolve. It also comes with a catch.

To enable you to effectively achieve this takes great practice and even more self-control. Often it takes a more highly-attuned state of presence to enable it, which you may argue defeats the purpose if the easier option is available to the same end. However, the mastery of this technique can be important for other events, particularly events that involve more people rather than one-on-one confrontations or disputes. Once in the domain of the already enlightened, this process can now be made available to all who understand and practice the process.

If in the process of Recognising the other's point of view you are not getting a clear picture, or there are too many people involved to gain a clear understanding, then ask your higher self to lift you out of your body so that you can gain a better, clearer viewpoint of the situation at hand. This is a technique often used by spiritual teachers in past life regression work to enable a patient to rise above difficult, scary, hard-to- understand memories of past life moments and give them a safe and emotion-free perspective on what was going on. This enables them to learn from the process

CHAPTER ELEVEN

as an outsider does when studying a case study in an educational context. The effect in the real-life process is the same.

By stepping outside of your body and rising above the situation, you can see (sometimes in slow motion) all that is going on around you, and that can often give you time to evaluate each of the key players and their viewpoints, as though you are looking through each of their eyes separately. If done properly, you can even slow time down enough to give you more time to Recognise and Reflect on the situation at hand, returning to your body with enough time to start diffusing the situation and Resolve it. Work with your spirit guides, the universe, or your God Source on this one. Practicing on everyday moments can be effective, even if they are not difficult or confrontational situations at first. But I do recommend that you practice as often as possible, as it is through repetition that effective use of the technique within confrontational situations becomes its most effective.

External Assignment

External Assignment is a process that is often done after the confrontational situation has passed but was not successfully Resolved. External Assignment is often utilised when the process of post-situational Reflection of the situation occurs and no understanding of the other person's point of view is available, even though the desire to have it resolved is still strong.

If you feel that a path towards Resolution is not available to you, or not clear, or you are too fatigued, too emotional, or incapable at the present time to resolve this issue, you can assign the problem to the universe to resolve. You literally explain to the universe that you cannot resolve this situation in your current state, and ask the universe to resolve the situation on your behalf, or provide the method and the appropriate time for you to resolve it effectively, and with love. I have always found that by saying it out loud it often results in a stronger intention, and therefore a more effective result.

This is a powerful technique of surrendering to the universe what you cannot deal with, releasing it from your energy field, and therefore releasing yourself of the Fear- based constructs that have consumed you to the point of distraction in the first place. Although a very effective technique for many reasons, I do not recommend you solely rely on this technique, because it has other impacts on your ability to use your voice, stand in your power, and confidently deal with situations from a position of Love.

So to wrap this up: through breathing to calm the body and to enable the mind to focus on the present, you can work through the well-practiced three-step process of:

CHAPTER ELEVEN

Recognise - understanding what Fear-based constructs are arising within you, as well as putting yourself in the other person's shoes to better understand their point of view and what Fear-based constructs are arising in them; **Reflect** - to utilise the information gleaned from the Recognition process to formulate a Love-based response, and to prepare yourself and your state of mind for implementing the Love-based response; and

Resolve - the implementation of your Love-based response, including discussing what mechanisms, rules or boundaries can be established to ensure a repeat of the situation doesn't occur again.

You use this process to associate, disarm and eradicate Fear-based constructs from your dealings with others (and eventually from your life entirely) and enable a love- filled, happy existence you call "life."

If you can practice this for three weeks, you can completely rewire any unhelpful habits you have built around your association to what is going on around you. Over three weeks you will replace any unhealthy habits, with new helpful associations.

If you keep practicing, you will not only become more efficient and effective in your application of it, but continued practice will develop it into an unconscious positive behavioural pattern that will continue to serve you for the rest of your life.

Once this is realised, real physical and mental healing will result, rebuilding the past's damage to your physical and mental conditioning. This is where true healing begins, and a life of pure peace and happiness is manifested into your everyday life experience.

On Earth as it is in Heaven.

Chapter Twelve

Four Thoughts to Ponder

I would like to discuss with you four key thoughts that I believe have shaped my path towards a healthier, happier and more evolved way of living. I offer these "Four Thoughts" as discussion points that will help you become more aware of yourself, how you perceive others, and how you interact with the universe around you.

In all the courses I teach, I try to explore these Four Thoughts in great detail because I believe the discussion creates a new perspective that enables a clearer way of thinking about others, our relationships, and what is ultimately important in our relationship with the universe around us. I believe that these Four Thoughts, explored thoroughly with others, enable everyone to understand themselves with more clarity.

The first of these Four Thoughts has been touched upon earlier in this book:

"Nobody does anything wrong - given their take on the world." What this statement means is that every single person that has ever lived on this planet justifies in some way that their actions are right, or part of the overall balance that makes up the universe as we know it. Mostly this justification is happening at an unconscious level as people go about their daily lives; but ultimately, everybody believes their perspective is the right perspective, because it is the only one they can experience. Of course, everything is just a matter of perspective. One person's "right" is another person's "wrong" and each believes their own perspective to be true. One person's Freedom Fighter is another person's Terrorist. Nobody does anything wrong given *their* take on the world.

To clarify this: I am not talking about the laws of the land, the compliance with those laws or the process associated with the judgement of one's actions against those laws. Society has commonly agreed that humans need some behavioural baseline of which to determine how the collective should act on a day-to-day basis. The laws that are put in place have an agreed structure, and it is also commonly agreed that a group of officers is needed (that

CHAPTER TWELVE

are sworn to a specific code of conduct) to police these laws on behalf of the people. Another smaller group of individuals are given the role of judgement, not to determine whether an individual has met a moral code, but to determine whether they have displayed a set of actions or behaviours that fit within the boundaries of that legal framework.

I am not referring to right and wrong in the legal judgement against the laws of the land. I am referring to a moral code that is within each and every one of us - a moral code that is very personal to each of us. Society has judges and police to administer our laws, and even if we don't agree with every detail of those laws or every application of the policing of those laws, we do understand the application and the process of that system. Moral codes are different. They are personal. Often as unique as we are. We all have a right to determine what is our moral code, and inasmuch as we are all unique, so are our thoughts, our feelings and our moral code of personal beliefs.

Just because someone has a different set of morals, doesn't mean that person *is* right. Nor does it mean they are wrong. In fact, I strongly believe there is only your opinion - based on your perspective - and someone else's opinion - based on their perspective. Your opinions, your morals and ethical positions are based on your upbringing, your past experiences and whatever new belief structures you have developed throughout your life. To be clear, I don't believe anyone has a right to negatively impact another person's life experience. I believe our own actions should never harm another. I believe our actions come from our thoughts, and therefore we shouldn't have thoughts that might harm another. Can I always achieve that every day? No. But it is a belief I have and that belief helps guide me on a path that *I* believe is right. My beliefs are not your beliefs. You are welcome to consider what I say in this book, and if it resonates with you, make it part of your belief system. That is your choice, and I will respect your right to make that choice. Irrespective of the outcome.

Humanity has constructed its own rules. This isn't because of God. God isn't a vengeful, judgemental God. God does not, and never has, stipulated that one thing is right and another is wrong. Humans created the set of rules and value sets society lives by today. Different religions (influenced by various cultural differences from land to land) took those human-created rules and interpreted them as God's instructions to humanity. God isn't judgemental. God doesn't need to be. God has only ever loved. Judgement is a fear-based construct and not one that God needs to entertain. Humans created judgement. Humans created right and wrong. Humans have decided that we need rules, structure and laws in place to protect people and to create a set of values to

CHAPTER TWELVE

guide how people should behave. Based on humanity's performance to date, we were right. We do need the rules. But where I think the application has gone awry is that we all think we are the policemen of our moral code. We believe for some insane reason that we are here to enforce our own personal moral code upon those around us.

Inasmuch as we might all agree that the Government cannot tell us what to think, what to feel or what to believe, that same Government cannot dictate to us what our own personal moral code is. It simply doesn't work that way. Yes, people can, and have, structured their own personal moral code on the aspects of the common laws that they feel most aligned with, but that is a choice we still have, and exercise on a daily basis.

We each have our own moral code. We each have the free will to decide on what makes up that moral code. That moral code helps us determine whether our actions are right or wrong. It keeps us honest, as individuals. That is the way it is and the way I believe it is meant to be. But in understanding this, we can at least agree that everyone's moral code is different, and it is allowed to be. This is what creates the difference in one person's belief, or justification of their thoughts, feelings and actions. In this we can understand why nobody does anything wrong, given their take on the world. Given their belief system. Given their moral code.

FREE FROM FEAR

The fact remains that an individual will believe that what they are doing is right; and if they at any point doubt it, they will create an argument within their own constructs that justifies their thoughts, actions or behaviours. People do this on a daily basis about many different things – to justify what they consume, to support their judgements of others, to support the policies or decisions they make, to strengthen their own belief systems, or to ensure they are not proven wrong about something. People rewrite history to support their decisions; they do it at a personal level, at a public level and at a global level. Every day. Everyone does it.

This is why one person's recollection of a long-term relationship is different to the other - in fact, why one person's recollection of anything is different to another. Different perspectives. We are not just viewers of our life experience, we are also projectors. We view what happens around us, interpret it based on our thoughts, feelings and belief structures (which are created by our past experiences), and project it outwards through our statements and actions. That interpretation gets filtered through us - and if we are present in a state of Love, the projection becomes a statement of that love presence. However, that is rarely the case. More often than not, the ego is present, constantly filtering everything we experience as a construct of its master: Fear.

CHAPTER TWELVE

Ultimately it is all an Ego-driven, masterful tool to create separation, division and disconnection. Why? Because the Ego needs to do it to survive. To simply exist. I am not here to judge you and your position of morality or your ethical standpoint. You are completely free to decide your own belief systems. God is not here to judge. The universe doesn't judge, it just responds. God created the universe to experience life through you, and me, and everyone and everything else for that matter. God does not judge because God knows we are all different. Different by design, and deliberately so. God loves us for that precise fact: because we are different, just the way it was intended to be.

Experience cannot happen if we are all the same. Then there would be no opposites to enable the ability to experience. We are not designed to be the same; we are designed to be different. We look differently, think differently, feel differently, experience differently, and we justify our decisions differently. We act given our take on the world, based on a wide-ranging, different set of circumstances that led us all to this point in time. We justify everything we believe and every action we take because of those belief structures. We judge everyone for being different, we judge everyone for making different decisions to us, and we judge everyone for having different beliefs or different thoughts.

The fact remains, we are different. We are all designed to be different - to look differently and to act differently. That is the point. We are all designed to think differently and to have different belief structures and make different choices. You have a right to free will. So does everyone else.

It has to be the most hypocritical, absurd human behaviour on the planet to judge someone for being what they were born to be - to judge someone for doing and thinking what they were born to do or think. Madness, is what it is. The Ego personified. Judging someone for being or acting differently to us!

Nobody does anything wrong given their take on the world. With that in mind, is your judgement of their choice any more right or wrong than their choice that you're judging them for? Is it your role to be their judge, jury and executioner? Then why be? Is it not just your Ego at play, running amok? They may have, in their mind, very good reasons for why they chose to act that way. Do you know their thoughts and belief structures, their moral code? Have you sat down and talked to them about it all? I would guess not. If it is not for God to judge then it is not for you to judge. Judgement is a Fear-based construct that only adds Fear-based energy into your life, and possibly theirs also. How does that help you, or them? It doesn't.

I want to be clear about something here. This was a belief that I have over-analysed for many, many years. It is something that I

CHAPTER TWELVE

struggled with because of the belief system I had been brought up with. I am not saying the belief system I was brought up with was bad, I am just saying that I realised that it was no longer serving me. I don't believe anyone has a right to negatively impact another person's life experience. I believe our own actions should never harm another. I believe our actions come from our thoughts, and therefore we shouldn't ever have thoughts that might harm another. But that is my belief. I have no right to judge another.

Who am I to cast the first stone, when I'm not perfect myself? Who am I to say someone else's decision is right or wrong? I am not. It is really that simple. I say, "Live and let live," which means let others live the life they choose to live. Every choice we make has consequences. The consequence delivers either pain or pleasure. We are not the universe's mechanism to deliver pain or pleasure to someone as the consequence of their decisions. That is the universe's job; let the universe sort that out.

By understanding this we can learn to allow others to live and not concern ourselves with something that isn't ours to deal with. In the process save ourselves from a lot of angst and negative energy as a result.

Even the paedophile who sexually interfered with me as a teenager, and then dumped me when he was done, justified what he was doing. Even his family justified to themselves that his choices were O.K. - not because they were paedophiles too, but because they loved him, for who he was; their brother, or their son. Yes, what he did to me had a long-lasting and hurtful impact on my life, but it also was instrumental in making me the strong soul that I sought to be. His actions were no different to the schoolyard bullies that called me a faggot; no different to a neighbour that screamed abuse and attacked me because I dared have an alternative opinion. All brought me to this point, enabled me to become the strong soul I am today.

If we can accept that no one does anything wrong, given their perspective, given their justification, and given their right to free will to choose their life experience, we can start to understand the beauty that is the universe. We don't need to judge others, and we don't need to consume our thoughts with what others are doing and whether it is right or wrong. They are just Fear-based thoughts that will never serve us. What we need to concern ourselves with is: What are *our* actions and thoughts? What choices are they leading to and how are they serving us... and others?

I believe that the vast majority of fear comes from our choices. If we choose a path of judgement of others - what they are doing, what beliefs they may or may not have - then what comes from our choices is reflected back at us. Nothing a person does really has anything to do with *us*. It is never about *you* and them. Anything

CHAPTER TWELVE

they do, any choice, any thoughts they may or may not have is only ever about *them*.

That leads me to the second thought: **"Everything is between you and the universe."**

Everything you do, think and say is never between you and someone else. Ultimately, it is only ever between you and the universe. The same goes for them.

We now know that every thought we have sends a signal to the universe of what we wish to experience as our life. A thought that gains energy though a build-up of emotions only sends a stronger signal and amplifies it further. Our thoughts and feelings *create*.

Karma is not about the universe getting back at someone. The universe isn't judgemental. It doesn't say you have done something that was bad so I am going to do something back to you in return to teach you some sort of lesson. All it thinks is, "You signal what you desire through your thoughts and feelings, so I will deliver to you what you desire." That's all. It really is that simple.

You harm someone else and the universe sends someone to harm you. You yell at someone in the car park, judge someone for cutting in line at the supermarket, or gossip about someone you dislike. "Thank you!" says the universe, and without judgement, sends that same signal back to you for your own life experience.

FREE FROM FEAR

You are in a rush and can't get to where you want quickly enough, so the universe puts someone in your way. This happens to me all the time. But what also happens is when I am calm and unconcerned about when I arrive at my destination I get nothing but green lights. Every thought you have and every choice you make is received by the universe and sent back to you. It is the way the universe operates, to everyone and everything. It is a universal law.

In breaking this down we can learn to understand that judgement of someone else only impacts us, because the universe will only respond to us. If someone has done something wrong in your eyes the universe will sort it out. There is no need for you to get yourself all worked up and in a pickle over it. It serves no one at all - least of all, you. The universe is the ultimate mirror, reflecting everything back at us and back at others in the world, also.

How someone treats you is not about you; it is about them. How you react is about you. This is a simple philosophy that I believe enables people to see that not everything has the perspective that our Ego gives it. If someone wants to rant and carry on, let them be on their merry way. The universe will show them a mirror by returning the same actions back to them. It may not be immediate, but it always happens. Let it go and focus on

CHAPTER TWELVE

your own thoughts and feelings. You do have complete control over your life experience.

Focus not on what others do, but focus on what you can do for others. I went through a period some years ago of handing out money to people living on the street. I thought that it was something small I could do to help them experience a better day, a fuller stomach, and a feeling that someone does care. I would give them blankets for warmth on cold winter nights, buy them food, or take them out for a meal and a chat. At the time I didn't understand the thought that everything is between me and the universe, but I did start to recognise the synchronicities that flowed strong and fast from these altruistic acts.

For some months I would scrape together what I could and give out what I had. I always ended giving out more than I needed to, but what I failed to see at the time (mostly because I was not focused on what it gave me in return) were the signals I sent out to the universe, and how they were amplified and returned to me. I started receiving from the universe unexpected windfalls from really unexpected sources. Money would come from strange sources - large amounts, too; and it was all because I had created a very strong signal that I was wealthy enough to give my money away to others that desperately needed it the most. Still to this day I seek to amplify this signal to the universe because it is what I wish the universe to know me as. Our Thoughts, Statements and Actions create our life experience because it is between you and the universe. Anyone else's thoughts about you are irrelevant, because the universe only listens to you, about you. The universe listens to them, about them.

It is a key reason why I now teach people these principles, showing them that a life without fear is possible; that they can create the life they want, and that they just need to take their attention away from the Fear-driven, egoic ways, and offer Love to themselves, their lives, and the actions they create as a result. It's not because it makes the Angels sing and applaud loudly when we all get it right (although they do). It is because we all deserve abundance in our lives - we just need to accept that we do, in fact, deserve it. The universe only responds, never judges.

The third thought is more about who we are, or who we want to be. The answer to that question is simple: **"We are the sum of our Thoughts and Actions."**

A number of key people around the world want to provoke a simple thought process in people by asking, "When you arrive on your death bed, what do you want your life to be remembered as?" The purpose of this statement is ultimately to get people to think about whether they are fulfilling their life's dreams through their current actions, and to think about it now, while there is still

CHAPTER TWELVE

enough time to do something about it.

I think most people can understand the basic principle that we don't take physical possessions with us after we die; we only take with us our life experiences (or our memories, if you will). Thinking about this and our own mortality only gets us so far, so I would like to ask you to think about your current life and how you would like people to remember you currently. This is not about getting caught up with what others think of us; it is more of an analogy to help us assess whether we are living our life the way we wish we could, given the opportunity.

Everything the universe sees and responds to is through our thoughts and actions. People are the same way - they will see us through our thoughts and actions, too. Yes, they will put their spin on it; their perspective will cast a filter over what they see, but this is not about what they see in us. This is about us understanding how we project our own self-image.

A large part of us manifesting a great life is to determine what that means to us what is required to enable it to become a reality. A couple of years ago I knew in my heart that I wasn't living the life I wanted to be known by. I wasn't clear on what exactly that was at the time, but I knew the path I was on, the beliefs I had, and the actions I was taking as a result of my choices, weren't serving me - and certainly weren't what I wanted to be remembered by.

FREE FROM FEAR

I embarked on a process of self-analysis and rediscovery to determine conclusively what type of man I *did* want to be. It was an incredibly emotional journey for me; one that wasn't without pain, nor without strong emotional conflicts with the way I was leading my life experience. The simple fact remained: I needed to determine whose opinions mattered to me, and how I wanted to be remembered by them.

Three groups of individuals became immediately apparent: my partner, my sons and myself. There was no order of significance, because each had very different meanings to me, but all led to the one simple conclusion - my thoughts and my actions were not reflective of who I truly was. It didn't take a rocket scientist to then figure out some change was required within myself.

I spent months deliberating on what "who I truly was" meant. I wrote it all down, and then rewrote it. Several times. But finally the answer became clear. I then set about developing a set of beliefs to replace all the past beliefs that were not serving me, and developed a range of actions that would be required to develop who I wanted to be.

I am now free with my thoughts and actions, happily being the person I am, knowing that I am living the life I always wanted. Fear-free, full of loving relationships, and giving what I can to

CHAPTER TWELVE

those that need help understanding who they are and where they want to be. Ultimately, we are the sum of our thoughts and actions. That is exactly how we will be remembered when we die if we are remembered at all.

The fourth thought is: **"We are the only one responsible for our life experience."**

This is often a contentious issue, and as much as I don't mean to insult anyone's belief system, I do mean to get you thinking outside of your belief system. This statement is all about the way we interpret what happens around us and who is responsible for it all. I raise this issue because in my experience most people believe that those around them are responsible for what they experience in life, and that others control their experience - or at the very least, impact it negatively or positively. I would like to publicly state that I believe that to be complete rubbish.

I am the only being responsible for my experience of life. The paedophile who abused me wasn't responsible for my experience of life. The school yard bullies, the boss who sacked me, the neighbour who attacked me, the church who abused me further out of their own self-interest - none of them were in any way responsible for my experience of life... and I am a fool to think otherwise. I know my words are harsh and they are deliberately so.

The neighbour who attacked? Well, that is between them and

the universe, and the universe took care of that. The bully, the church and the boss, the universe handled all that, too. I may not have known the details of how the universe did it, but it was none of my business anyway. The thought that we are the only one responsible for our life experience is everything about the *perspective* we have towards our life and nothing about what actually *happens* to us. Yes, people may try to harm you with what they say, but that is about them, not you. Yes, some people may also try to harm you physically, but that is also about them, not you. What is important to your life experience is how you choose to make yourself feel about the situation that has happened. That is entirely within your control - even if dealing with a psychotic person feels like it isn't within your control, in the physical sense.

Your interpretation of the event, and how you structure your thoughts about it, is entirely within your control. You can choose to get all caught up in the moment, complain to all those around you as to how terrible it all was, and live in your pain body if you want. This is only attention-seeking behaviour at best and will never serve you. In fact, people who commonly take this approach will be offended by these words because they will genuinely believe that everything that isn't perfect in their life is absolutely someone else's fault - someone else, or something else, is always to blame.

The simple fact remains: you can blame someone else for their

CHAPTER TWELVE

actions effecting your life, or you can choose to see their actions as being all about them, and not let it in any way effect your state of happiness. This enables you to go on about your own way, to live your own life. *Recognise* it for what it is: *between someone else and the universe*. *Reflect* on what you choose to experience: *happiness and joy in realising that you are, in fact, O.K.* Then, *Resolve* it within yourself by taking action to experience it as something that serves you: *learn whatever needs to be learned from that experience*.

Your life experience is not about what happens to you; it is about what you choose to see in what happens to you, either as a reflection of you and your life or a reflection of something that is between someone else and the universe. Drama, self-pity and continuing the story of an event well after it has happened will never serve you. What will serve you is choosing constructs of Love in difficult situations to ensure the universe sends you back constructs of Love in return.

We are all responsible for our experience of our life. We are not responsible for anyone else's experience of their life, because *they* are responsible for their experience. The Ego will often try to drag you into someone else's drama because the Ego wants friends in its egoic conquering of you and your immediate environment. The Ego will try to enforce someone else's drama as your own, but you are too smart for that now; you can recognise another's drama when you see it. You can see another's Ego when it rears its ugly head to drag you in. Love it. Offer it love, but don't buy into the drama, for you will only add fuel to it. Loving it will dissipate it and calm them down. Their drama is not yours to own, nor to take on board. They are responsible for their life experience through the thoughts and actions they take as a result of the environment they find themselves in.

Please remember that nobody does anything wrong given their take on the world. Their actions are between them and the universe anyway. We are all the sum of our thoughts and actions, and we are solely responsible for our own life experience.

Be happy, because it is who *you* truly are.

ANDREW HACKETT

Four Thoughts

Nobody does anything wrong - given their take on the world.

Everything is between you and the universe.

We are the sum of our Thoughts and Actions.

We are the only one responsible for our life experience.

AndrewHackett.com.au

Cut this page out and put it on your fridge, cork board or on your workplace desk to provide a quick reference and reminder when you may need it the most.

Chapter Thirteen

The Link Between Your Uniqueness and Your Purpose in Life

Many great minds believe that prior to being born in this world we set out a plan on everything we (as the soul) wish to accomplish in this physical lifetime. To our soul – who we truly are - the purpose of incarnating into this lifetime is all about personal growth and spiritual development towards an ultimate state of pure enlightenment. Our soul evolves through the understanding gained from the many and varied experiences gathered from multiple lifetimes. This collection of lifetimes is often referred to as our past lives.

I also share this belief. I believe we travel the cosmos in search of opportunity from one lifetime to the next to experience as much about life as it can possibly offer. With this comes the understanding that we don't live or die (in the human understanding of the concept), but that our life as the soul is eternal and we endlessly move from one form to another, experiencing everything we possibly can. Much like water; in the cold, water becomes solid; in extreme heat, a gaseous form; at room temperature, a liquid.

We live on eternally, moving from one state of the non-physical (the spiritual state), to a physical state of living inside a body (being born into this lifetime). When we die (so to speak) we – our soul – doesn't die at all, because the soul is eternal. We move from the physical state, living inside the body, back to the non-physical state (leaving the body behind to "go to heaven"). We all know of this process at some level, but over the millennium we have been taught different understandings of this process, depending on the culture or environmental belief systems we were born into.

Before we arrive, the idea is that we put together our lifetime plan. This is an ideal path that will hopefully enable us to experience what we seek to experience for the purposes of spiritual growth and personal development at a soul-based level. We enlist

CHAPTER THIRTEEN

the souls of those we are choosing to incarnate with - the parents we choose to be born to, and the siblings, friends and lovers we choose to experience this life with - in the hope that they will be able to create the events in our lives that stimulate the growth needed. This helps us either stay on our pre-chosen path, or to experience the life we seek to experience through lifetime's free-will choices.

Now, this may seem a little bit weird to you, and I am afraid it is going to get a little bit weirder. But before we go there, let's park this concept and discuss another, before we come back to link the two together.

I think we all readily accept the idea that we, as humans, are all unique. If you ever look at two human beings you see that they are different in one way or another, even if on the surface they appear to look the same, act the same, or have the same belief systems. As a collective observation, any one person will always be different to any other person you may care to compare them with. As individuals, there are so many different possible variables that there really is no way two people could possibly be the same. The universe not only wants it this way, but it is an essential part of humanity and part of the universe's plan for all of us.

So in accepting the fact that we are all unique, I see that there are two main questions (possibly more) that come from that fact.

FREE FROM FEAR

If we are all unique, why are we unique and for what purpose?

I believe we all come to this great planet called Earth to serve a particular purpose. I believe these purposes are as wide and varied as we all are. I believe there is no "right purpose" and no "wrong purpose," inasmuch as there is no right or wrong, given an individual's perspective of their own existence.

Our purpose is predetermined by us, at the soul-based level, prior to coming into physicality through birth. Part of the deal that comes with the physical world existence is that we will forget what our purpose is and have to figure it out along the way - hopefully before it is too late to do anything about it. Most people I come across daily know deep down that they have a purpose for being here, but they honestly have no idea what that purpose was.

I struggled with this notion, feeling for years like a superhero with no cause. I knew from a young age that I have a very specific purpose on this planet, but I couldn't put my finger on even the beginning of it for some 40 years. Not knowing your purpose can be quite stressful for some people, as they search endlessly for it, not knowing that they are manifesting the counter product of what they desire.

I say there is a very good reason why people feel there is a greater reason for being on this planet. I believe it is because they are right. Their intuition, the cellular-based response to their soul's

CHAPTER THIRTEEN

communication through their heart is telling them as loudly as it can, that what they are doing day-to-day is not the path they chose prior to arriving in this physical lifetime. This realisation can be hard to hear, and often we don't want to know. Like taking the "red pill" in the movie *The Matrix*, we cannot go back from that realisation. What we now know cannot be un-known. We cannot go back to living a life of ignorant bliss once we accept that we are not fulfilling our soul's purpose in this life.

Now I want to counsel you at this point to be careful with the understanding. I believe it is not an answer that arrives with a bang, but the answer is carefully scripted from birth. I believe that everything that happens to us is part of the universe's magic to gently steer us back on course towards that ultimate purpose. The answer comes through extensive searching, listening and quiet reflection. I believe the answer is in the understanding of why we are unique.

To understand this I think we need to explore our uniqueness and what makes us unique. I think most would believe it all comes from our parents, the genetic makeup created by the conception that brings us into this life. I don't disagree with this thought, but I suggest it is just the beginning of the process overall. We are born with a unique set of characteristics that are both from our genetic make-up and from our upbringing and collective life experience.

FREE FROM FEAR

This latter part of our makeup is vital to understanding our purpose.

Through our birth we are given a fundamental set of building blocks of which to build from. We learn our behaviours and often, our persona, from our parents and the siblings we live with from a young age. As we grow we develop our belief systems from people we trust and admire the most in our lives. As we move through our teenage years we start to challenge some of those beliefs. Our bodies change, our attitudes change, and our desire for understanding changes. As we process this mostly unconscious change within our lives, the collective experiences impact us more and more, until, as young adults, we have already started to create our own set of beliefs. I believe what we experience throughout our lives is provided by the universe to shape us into the people we need to be to deliver on the purpose we pre-scripted prior to our incarnation. Sometimes this arrives as a positive influence in our lives as much as it happens through the negative experiences. Understanding them is often difficult, specifically when it throws us into Fear-based constructs that overpower our day-to-day living. Stopping, breathing and listening to our intuition, albeit very difficult to do (especially when we don't know how or why we need to) is important for us to tap into the explanation as to why it happened.

CHAPTER THIRTEEN

As we now know, our intuition talks in whispered tones. Our inner guidance is our soul's communication through our heart, and it is gentle and reassuring. If we are living a life based on Fear's constructs and the Ego's controls, a life of loud expressions and complex and constant interruptions, the universe and our soul's messages need to think of other ways to enable us to learn, shape and guide us towards our chosen path. Our soul wants us to listen. Sometimes when we are new to this understanding we need to sit quietly and listen to what our soul is trying to say. Turn the music and the television off, stop fretting about work and the kids, stop judging others with ridiculous manufactured stories that the world is out to get us. If we don't understand the power of how synchronicities work in our lives we can often overlook them or ignore them. I trust enough to let you know that the universe is intent on you getting the message. It will never give up trying to get you to listen.

In my experience it is nearly impossible to hear it until you make a simple choice. If you don't want to listen, or you don't understand enough to know that you even need to listen, it is nearly impossible - impossible to make such a choice. The choice is essential, as represented by that "red pill" from *The Matrix*. There have been numerous representations of it in modern culture for centuries before and since.

FREE FROM FEAR

The choice is… that you commit to the desire to change, that you decide that it is time to make the required changes in your life. That is honestly all it takes. I promise you it is the single most powerful decision you will ever make in your life. When you do, the universe will rejoice, your angels will applaud loudly, and mountains will move at your feet to enable you to listen.

Yet, as we listen, we need to understand that the truth is often hard to hear. Sometimes the belief systems we were raised with are not working for us anymore, and we need to start again. We need to create a new set of belief systems that will enable us to listen to the way the universe wants to communicate. It isn't easy, and it is often foreign to us. But the yearning for the truth is real, because our heart knows that what we currently know isn't the truth we need to hear.

I just want to pause here and let some of this sink in before I push you further. I know you are ready for it, but I just want to make sure you know you are ready for it.

I want to list out what we have covered so far in this chapter, to consolidate before moving on.

- Before we are born, we put together a plan of what we want to experience in this life so that we can grow and develop as our soul, to travel on the path towards understanding and enlightenment.

CHAPTER THIRTEEN

- When we write our plan, we enlist – at a soul-based level – the others that we will experience this life with, to help us experience what we set out to experience, good or bad.

- Soon after birth, we start to forget why we are here and the physical-world experience starts to become more real than the reality of where we came from and why we came.

- We are all unique - and for very good reason. Our uniqueness comes from our foundational baseline, from our genetic makeup, and from our upbringing, our family, peers and collective life experiences.

- Our intuition is the language of our heart; it speaks in hushed tones, and only speaks in the language of Love. Everything that comes from our soul, through our heart, uses the language of Love.

If we can understand some of these basic principles we can possibly explore it a little further and a little deeper to enable us to close out the loop.

When we live in the spiritual state, the state of the non-physical, we can know all there is to know. Time is not linear and all knowledge is omnipresent. At this point we can foresee the life we wish to lead and the experiences we need to be able to lead it, as we also understand the limitations of the physical world and how it operates. Everything the soul does is for the experience of the growth that life provides.

For those of you that have done some past life regression therapy you will understand that most of us have been through many different lifetimes and that these lifetimes have taken many different paths. Some we relate to as good or righteous paths; others are morally questionable or downright evil. But all is done, as is this lifetime, for the soul's purpose of understanding and experiencing all that life has to offer, without judgement. The purpose for these different life decisions is that the soul offers itself for many purposes - sometimes for our own personal growth, and other times for the personal growth of other people. It is part of the commitment we make at many different levels for the overall evolution of our soul family and the soul collective.

We must keep in mind that all matters of the soul are matters of Love and in the spirit of Love for all souls and beings. This is where it can be difficult for some to move forward.

As our life is pre-scripted, by us, with the omnipresent knowledge of how it will all play out, and everything that ever happens to us is an act of Love and for our greater good (even if only at a soul-based level), then we can deduce that we have nothing to fear and that we are eternally safe from everything we previously thought could harm us. Remember, Fear does not want

CHAPTER THIRTEEN

you to know the truth because then it will make itself irrelevant. The soul can only speak the truth, part of the language of Love. I know the consequences of this statement are hard to grasp for some. But please let me explain.

I had a good childhood; beautiful by anyone's standard. As a teenager I started to explore the development of my own belief systems. This left me vulnerable and open to manipulation, but it also opened the doors to the experience I needed to shape who I am today. As with all matters of the soul, how we structure our life and its purpose to help us find our uniqueness and our path is ultimately up to us. Only we can create our life, either through setting out our path and co-conspirators before we incarnate, or through our life decisions once we are alive. No one else can create our life experience. I believe I could not have found the understanding I needed to develop down the paths necessary for me to be who I am today if it wasn't for my abuser, my perspective from what I experienced as a result of his actions, and every act I have experienced from that point until now.

I believe that the truly terrible things that happen to us in our lives are nothing more than an opportunity to become stronger and wiser and more compassionate to ourselves and those around us. The need to resolve our pain starts with forgiving ourselves, because that is the place where shame and guilt is resolved. I believe that these key events in our lives develop our uniqueness and are the key to what we are here to do, and why. If we are unique, and our path is also unique – essential to the ongoing workings of the universe – it only fits that our uniqueness is the imperative ingredient to our unique purpose.

Through my decision in 2007, long after the abuse event, to explore a path of personal growth and development (rather than allowing a path of self-destruction through allowing Fear-based constructs to develop and take hold), I was able to fix myself. I started a process (albeit unconsciously at the time) to create the version of myself that was necessary to set about discovering why I am here. This process also enabled me to develop the strengths and understanding necessary to be able to take action on my purpose. That, in turn, enabled me to help those around me to seek and develop the necessary growth within them to find their paths and take action on their purpose.

It is important to understand that like the jigsaw puzzle in my awakening process, each piece played an integral role in the current result. It stands to reason that, like the people that helped shape my life – either directly or indirectly – so your life, and the actions you take on a daily basis, also influence the lives of others, whether you understand it or not.

Through this understanding we can start to accept that the

CHAPTER THIRTEEN

pain and suffering we have experienced as a result of the actions of others is an opportunity for growth and development.

I'm not saying that what may have happened to you, or what has happened to the millions of people in the world's history to date, isn't awful, disgusting and nearly impossible to live through (and for some it *has* been impossible to live through). What I am saying is that all of it was, in one way or another, part of our individual and collective journey, to enable us to learn, to grow and to love each other in the way our souls know we deserve to love and be loved. I am saying that the history of wrongs throughout human evolution show us that growth is necessary to enable us to evolve (at an individual and a collective level) to a higher state of love-based consciousness that we all seek within our hearts.

I say, what we see as tragedy, is in fact a blessing. It is hard work. It feels impossible at times, and will crush us if we allow it too to control us through the ego and Fear- based constructs. But if we can have the presence of mind to accept in every moment, that *this* moment is going to provide us an opportunity to make a stronger and more capable version of ourselves, then nothing can harm us. Nothing can hurt us, *ever*. Every experience immediately benefits us. This is a secret of highly conscious beings.

I know the loss of a loved one feels impossible to understand at the time. I know a tragedy of the permanent disablement of someone we care for seems impossible to cope with at the time. I know that war, and the casualties of war, seem impossible to understand on every level, if we look at them as they first appear.

I believe they are the exact opportunity we need, the exact opportunity the universe is providing, and the exact opportunity humanity requires to wake us all up from the fear- driven, disconnected slumber, and get us to understand and realise that we are all here for a purpose, and it is our purpose that enables another to realise theirs.

If any of the authors of the hundreds of books I have read over the last five years alone had not found their purpose, through hardship and growth, they would not have written their book to send me the message I needed at the precise time the universe knew I would need it. When a book wasn't available to give me the message I needed to hear, the universe sent me a person to give me the message face-to-face. The universe provided every opportunity I needed to arrive at the exact point I needed to be. Even if it was the screaming neighbour, furious at some decision I may have rightfully made; or a jealous friend, angry at me for some reason; or my abuser, taking what he believed was his to take. I believe that they are all provided by the universe for good reason, because there was some opportunity for growth or personal development that

CHAPTER THIRTEEN

was somehow deemed necessary. I believe if you ask any person that has risen from great personal tragedy, or overcome great personal hardship in their lives, that they will say that the tragedy, hardship or key traumatic events that occurred in their past, was *instrumental* to making them the stronger, more capable person you see before you.

I am no exception to this rule, and I don't believe you are either. Nobody is put in our life without a reason, whether they are there for one minute or for your whole life. Everybody plays a role in creating the uniqueness that is what we are for the purpose of enabling us to find our path and be strong enough to take action on it.

Although I may not have chosen to be abused, like nobody chooses to be raped, beaten or psychologically abused, I can however, choose to see it as an opportunity for growth and great personal development. I can choose, at any given time, how to create my life experience from the events that have occurred in my life.

As I said before, if we can have the presence of mind to accept in every moment, that *this* moment is going to provide us an opportunity to make a stronger and more capable version of ourselves, then nothing can harm us. *Ever.* We have complete control to ensure by our own choice, that every experience can immediately benefit us.

I am not here to do what you are here to do. You are not here to do what I am here to do. Our paths are as unique as we are. And, if by some beautiful magic, we both appear on the same path, it is only because our souls decided the message needed more disciples to speak it. The universe is intelligent in its design and this intelligence is not only all around us, it is us.

Just like the four days of my awakening, and the visualisation that appeared before me showed me: every single event that occurred in my life (and in others' lives that touched mine) was deliberately orchestrated to enable me to learn what I needed to learn, to enable me to grow and to develop into the being you see before you now. If those people didn't do what they did, didn't write the books that I read, didn't yell and scream at me, or abuse me when they did, I would not have created the uniqueness to write the book you read here before you.

Just like my life was shaped through the events that occurred since my birth, yours has also been. It is already being sculpted, and has been for some decades. I will go so far as to say that your life is so important to the success of Humanity's awakening that generations of actions have been carefully taken to ensure you appeared here, book in hand, at this precise time. The angels that got Michelle and I together, that taught me what I needed to know

CHAPTER THIRTEEN

to speak to you now, are also your angels - and they watch over you every day. You are never alone. Especially in hard times. They know the traumas of your life are making you the unique *you* that your soul, your angels and the universe knows you need to be to fulfil the life you set out for yourself before you arrived here. They know how important your path is. They inspire these words in the hope you may also believe it, too.

But whether you believe this or not is (to be honest with you) *irrelevant*. It is happening already, and has been for decades, if not generations.

However, when you accept it, and allow your belief systems to change to accommodate this understanding, you will start to understand a few key things:

- Everything that you have experienced in life has occurred for your greater good.

- Nothing can harm you. Everything that happens to you actually happens to assist your personal growth as a spiritual being.

- Your ego has been lying to you all along, albeit to maintain its own existence.

FREE FROM FEAR

- Everything you believed that was holding you back needs to be re-thought.

- Your fears are nothing but an ego-created illusion, and actively working to overcome them proves this beyond all reasonable doubt.

- Understanding and accepting your uniqueness is essential to finding your purpose and predetermined journey in this life; and

- That same unique you… is your message to the world.

Andrew Hackett

Everything I experience in my life
is for my greater good.

Nothing can harm me; every experience
is to assist my personal growth.

My ego only tells me *lies* about my life experience.
My fears are an ego-created *illusion*.

I have *NO* limitations.

My Uniqueness is directly related to
my purpose in life.

My Uniqueness is my message to the world.

AndrewHackett.com.au

Cut this page out and put it on your fridge, cork board or on your workplace desk to provide a quick reference and reminder when you may need it the most.

Chapter Fourteen

Before You Run Off to Save the World...

I would like to part with another thought that I believe is seldom addressed in today's spiritual revolution. I often find judgement in the eyes of spiritual people because they believe they have a right to judge because they have experienced an awakening of some variety.

I would like to say that it is not your job to point out to people, strangers or even friends or family, that their Ego is present and that they need to shut it down or resolve the issues that it brings into their lives. It is not your job to tell them they have to wake up, and realise what is going on. You are not here to tell anyone what is wrong with their lives, their behaviour or their actions. It just simply isn't, because to do so is the incarnation of your own ego,

FREE FROM FEAR

forcing a Fear-based construct of judgement upon another.

If they come to you asking for your help - and they will, when they feel you being present – then that is your opportunity to explain the concepts you have learned from this book, or from your own life experience. When they reach out looking for answers that is your chance to show them the reality of the world around them. But please do so from your own state of presence; then you will do so from a position of Love and not judgement. To do otherwise is only communicating with them through your own Ego and it will further inflame theirs. You manifest what you put out, and your Ego always loves company. You would end up manifesting their Ego with yours. Instead, I say manifest their Love, with judgement-free presence.

Explain to them the concepts of the ego, how it works and why, from a judgement-free, unconditional Love point of view. That may stop their Ego from interfering in the process because darkness cannot survive in the presence of light - but only if they are seeking the answer. The unconditional Love offered through your teaching will dissipate the existence of their ego, open up the channels between you and them, and allow the process of remembering within them, because their own presence will connect them with their own inspiration. That is what the good spiritual teachers do.

CHAPTER FOURTEEN

A good spiritual teacher teaches through the channels of inspiration of the student, as it is the student's inspiration that truthfully knows what the student needs to hear. Some teachers use their own egoic-influenced judgement to decide on what a student needs to hear. A good teacher listens, at a soul-based, cellular level to what the student needs.

I believe that is why so many spiritual teachers lose their way. They start off in the right way but lose it over time. When they start to lose it the Ego jumps in - mostly unconsciously to them - and starts to influence again as they try to get back what they feel they have lost. That is why Eckhart Tolle shows people that evangelizing the word of God is not the way to get the word across at all, because through the evangelizing there is strong judgement upon the listener that will certainly invoke their Ego into a Fear-based response (if it doesn't shut down the listener altogether). Eckhart shows us through leading by example. Through *being*. That is what we are here to do.

Evangelising the word of God is judgement at its core, which is a construct of Fear and is not a process of Love at all. It is often carefully masked as Love, but it isn't and cannot be. This is where the churches and the world's religions have it all wrong, and they know it. They need to control through fear, to put people in the pews, to get them to believe; so when they tell them to open their wallets, they do as they are told.

Please love all people, all living things. But I understand that people are the challenge because they don't love back like animals do, like the trees do, like your planet does. Despite what humans do to Mother Earth, she still loves back. Unconditionally. Every time.

We must all Love, and be Love. That is the key.

Change is only a thought away. This is the path that you and every human being is on. The vast majority just don't know it. Most never will until it is too late for them. Everyone and everything is living out the perfection that is life. It is never too late to *be* change. It is never too late to *be* Love.

Some months ago I made the decision to stop trying to be Spiritual. For years I searched for spirituality like it was destination. I thought I would arrive there and be able to finally say, "Hey, look at me. I am spiritual!"

It was only through my conscious decision to stop trying to be spiritual that I started being Spiritual. I decided to stop the search - the workshops, the conferences and the personal one-on-one sessions - and focus on my path: each step, each day, carrying the water and chopping the wood. It was only through this process that my presence allowed myself to be Spiritual. I made the choice to lead by example.

CHAPTER FOURTEEN

My journey may be recognised by many as the right path to take. It may also be judged as the wrong journey to take. Many will also not recognise it due to the limitations imposed by their own ego, and others because it isn't their truth. But that is their journey to walk, and that is O.K. Too many are trying to be something they are not. Too many are searching. Too many are trying to live someone else's idea of what the journey should look like. The finding is not in the searching, it is in the being. In the Now.

The simple process of searching may open the eyes. It may in fact awaken, as it did with me many years ago now. But it will never deliver you to spirituality. The simple idea of searching is a belief of separation, that what you need is out there, somewhere. Outside of you.

There is no separation. *There is no Separation!!!*

Not from me. Not from others. Not from the animals, the birds or the fish. Not from the trees, the bees or the Earth. Not from the natural or the man-made. Not from you, not from God.

So please, please don't evangelise. Teach those who come to hear your word. Love those who don't, and offer unconditional love to those who throw stones at you. This was what made Jesus great. Like Buddha, he conquered the Ego once and for all but was never arrogant enough to ever think that he had. Even in his execution he loved his tormentors. This is what he meant by turning the other cheek. Love those that strike out at you, for that is when love is at its greatest, strongest and most undeniable. It is at this precise moment that the world will start to change... on Earth, as it is in heaven.

* * * *

Any process you decide to focus on for personal growth and development will be greatly enhanced by looking after yourself better. Science has proved many times over the direct connection between the mind and the body. Medical science knows of the power the mind has over the body, and the negative effects manifested in the body as a result of an unhealthy mind. The creation of disease in the body is often attributed to the condition of the mind, as much as it is also attributed to what we consume and how well we look after our body. This goes both ways: the body can also impact the mind, if it is feeling unwell and not well-looked after. It is a two-way street. Although this book is about looking after our state of mind, we also need to look after our body. It all goes hand in hand.

I highly recommend that you give the following five key points some food for thought.

CHAPTER FOURTEEN

1. *Stay present.* This is the most important of all factors. Practice it, live it, be it. Your presence is the key to everything in your life, your success, your abundance and your personal growth. Don't forget to breathe. This will always bring you back to yourself, your inspiration and your soul. This will enable you to better understand the processes in this book and will give you more energy. Some people believe that proper breathing will improve your health and help your body regenerate each day.

2. *Make sure you get plenty of quality sleep.* Good sleep is imperative and also a great tool towards freeing yourself of Fear. Proper rest and relaxation is important towards looking after yourself. Proper rest helps us maintain a healthy heart and a healthy mind. Good rest makes it easier for us to identify when the ego is present. Whenever the body is deprived of its essential requirements it impacts the mind and our ability to manage our day-to-day matters.

3. *Look after your body.* You need to maintain the body you have for as long as possible. You need to keep your body going, and going well. To do that, you need to look after it better. This involves learning about what dietary limitations your body has and eating more fruit and vegetables, as well as more unprocessed forms of natural food. Think about the impact that alcohol has on your system. I used alcohol to disconnect

and forget, and it certainly did its job at that very well. Try cutting alcohol out entirely, and make note of the positive affects you experience as a result. Try more exercise and consider activities like yoga and meditation. Oh, and don't forget to drink more water, it is essential to good health.

4. *Love. Love. Love.* Focus on your Love Presence. Stay present and breath and it will all come to you. Have no fear by offering it Love. Be love. Live and let live. Love and let Love. Love others the way you wish to be loved, with passion and joy in your heart. Treat every situation with the question, "What would love do?", "What would my soul do?" or, "What can I do that brings love into this situation?"

5. *Have Faith.* Faith in who you are, what you are doing, where you are going and why you are here. Faith is what got you to this point, and it is what will get you to where you want to be. Faith is everything in the mind of the lover. Faith creates life, faith delivers love, and faith is what enables you to achieve everything you could ever achieve. Faith is limitless. You are limitless.

Always remember that the journey is not a path to travel, but is a point within oneself. It is all there, already. You just need to remember that it is. There is no one way to the mountaintop, and everyone has the right to decide their own path. You included.

CHAPTER FOURTEEN

I am my life's creator. I choose to create a happy life, full of laughter, fun and excitement. My life is the sum of my experiences, and I am the only one responsible for my experience of life. You can choose to create a happy life, and you are the only one who can. You are the only one responsible for your experience of your life. So make it the most amazing, most incredible, most loving life you can possible come up with. And then make it bigger than that. Shine, bright like the morning star.

I offer my life to be an example to all of you, of everything Love can be. Unconditional and without limits. I do love you, with all of my heart. Thank you for walking this journey with me. I have loved holding your hand. It is warm and soft.

It is time now for you to go on your way. Be brave and keep your faith. You are ready for everything Fear can throw at you. It is no longer your master. Morning is upon us and the cold dark night will soon be on its way. Like the early morning sun rises to offer us a new beginning, yours has just arrived. Today the sun shines just for you. Today is first day of the rest of your life. Choose Love. Love, that is unconditional and without judgement.

Please become an example to others, because by leading by example, we light the way.

Not for others to follow... but for them to see for themselves.

About the Author

ANDREW HACKETT has more than 20 years of experience helping people think outside their limitations and move beyond their fears so they can accomplish amazing things in their life, business, and relationships.

Download FREE Bonus Content:

http://AndrewHackett.com.au/FreeFromFearBonus

www.ingramcontent.com/pod-product-compliance
Lightning Source LLC
Chambersburg PA
CBHW071908290426
44110CB00013B/1323